MADE IN THE USA

An autobiography of fun things encountered so far

Robert "Bob" Miller

Copyright © 2017 Robert Miller

To contact the author email:
madeintheusabook@gmail.com

*Dedicated to the family and friends,
who have contributed to this book
knowingly or unknowingly.*

Contents

Chapter One:

A New Beginning

Lucky Kansas, I've arrived on borrowed money

Born 18 December 1928 – Bob the Bumbler

Borrowed Money

I was born in Kansas City Mo. St. Josephs hospital, and transported home in the arms of my Aunt Hattie since Dad had to borrow hospital money from her which was about $56.00. I flirted, and she fell for me and proclaimed that I would become rich and famous. This prophesy turned out to be an eminent prediction of my later years as you will see-------

This is an especially good birthday since it is exactly 7 days before Christmas day and then in 7 more days to New Year's day. This has enabled me to enjoy three whole weeks of celebrating in the dead of winter. Incidently, just a few weeks before me, a mouse was born (Mickey) and he has becume a bit more famous than me. But I'm not done yet!

First Home, Olatha Kansas

My Mom ran a little grocery store by the railroad tracks and it's where we lived in a room upstairs while Dad, Uncle Harry and Aunt Hattie worked as field hands for a big farmer. The store didn't belong to us, and it was sort of a "work for rent" arrangement. The railroad had some Mexican workers that lived in box cars nearby and some of the Mexican ladies helped baby sit with me while Mom had the store open. My Aunt Hattie didn't trust them and she raised a fuss with Mom several times, claiming that the Mexicans might kidnap me for money since they thought we owned the store and had money.

Early launguage

1929 I spent a lot of time with these Mexican ladies while Mom tended store. I think I may have learned some Spanish at that time, but it has since been forgotten I suppose. No! not quite *"Adios Amigo"* is still there.

A bolt of lightning hit the tin roof of the store one night which rattled all of us out of bed. A heavy rain came right after and put out a fire which was just in one little spot. We went back to bed, next day was nice sunshine and Mom opened the store as usual and Dad went off to work on the store owners farm.

In the early afternoon a mexican lady entered the store screaming at the top of her lungs at mom about something. Mom thought she had a fire in her boxcar home, but after going outside she discovered that our entire room upstairs was engulfed in flames. She went back in, grabbed me and $6.83 from the money box and watched the entire store building burn to the ground.

I had nothing to do with that fire that distroyed everything we owned. We couldn't live with Uncle Harry and Aunt Hattie since they lived in a cattle barn belonging to their employer farmer. So we lived for a little while in a boxcar with the Mexican folks while Dad finished his harvest duties, but soon we were hitching rides to live with relatives in Illinois where none of those folks spoke Mexican.

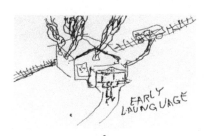

EARLY LAUNGUAGE

First Wealth

Soon thereafter a stockmarket crash took place and rich guys were jumping out of windows because they had no money anymore. Dad always joked that "lucky us" would have lost millions too if we hadn't been so poor. My Aunt Hattie had opened a bank savings account in my name and put $1.00 in it for me, but the money had to be withdrawn for travel expenses to Illinois.

My mom kept the little Savings account book because I think she fully intended to repay me when times got better. I found that little book many years later and always wondered what that savings account would have been worth some thirty years later.

Chapter Two:

Mom's Illinois "wer'e here"

Lucky Relatives

1930 - We had made it to Whitehall Ill (Moms hometown) and moved temporarily in with Grandpa and Grandma Taylor for a few days. My Dad couldn't stand Grandpa because he was a retired *"hellfire and damnation"* Baptist Preacher. Dad worked with my Uncle Irvin (moms brother) hand digging water wells and was able to rent part of a house with Mom's sister and Brotherinlaw. This was called a tenament building where several familys lived near a railroad track and I think I spent many hours looking and waiting for some of my Mexican friends to show up in one of the railroad boxcars.

A brother was born that year and we had begun to collect a few household items such as bedding, clothing and give away dishes. We had a foldaway bed and mattress given to us, but it was infested with bedbugs. Dad decided that we probably would be moving around quite a bit since work was hard to find, so he built a big box with rope handles at each end and a linolium top. This big box was to be used for moving belongings where ever we needed to go. Dad got a teamsters job since he was good with horses and mules, road building. We rented houses in Ill or lived with kind hearted relatives for the next several years since Dad worked whereever he could avoiding the landlord when necessary. The World depression was in full swing. I had nothing to do with that either.

Destructive Kid

I was about three years old when this frightful experience took place. It is probably the earliest childhood memory I can recall and is especially burned into my memory. We were living with my Uncle Francis and Aunt Fefa in Whitehall Illinois since the great world depression was in full swing and cohabitation was a crucial matter of survival. Mom and aunt Fefa baked biscuits about every other day or so in a cook stove fired with corncobs, to be eaten with fried potatoes on most days.

Incidentally most generally an evening meal consisted of a large bowl of fried potatoes placed in the middle of the table and kids (about four at that time) were served along with the men and the women ate last. After the big bowl was emptied, kids were allowed to soak up the cooking grease with day old biscuit halves wiped around the bowl bottom which was considered a supper treat.

This particular day we were out of baking powder. Mom volunteered to walk to the little neighborhood grocery store about half dozen blocks away so biscuits could be baked before the evening meal. I put up a fuss to go along with Mom since I was fascinated with all the various items on the shelves and tables of this one room grocery store in the middle of a residential neighborhood. The owner lived in the back room somewhere. He was a tall skinny bald headed guy wearing an apron that was always soiled according to Aunt Fefa. Mom held my hand as we walked to the store since some dogs at a couple of houses were always looking for somebody to threaten. I remember climbing the front steps into the store (about four) and into what was originally a porch now used as a display area for bags of bulk goods. But the best part was inside a front room having a long counter at one side with candies and suckers on sticks and was guarded by the tall guy. The rest of the room had shelves full of boxed and canned goods.

This day a special display had been set-up just inside the door consisting of a couple of wood shipping boxes covered with wrapping paper. On top of this was tin cans of pork & beans (I think) stacked in pyramid style taller than me. My mom was engaged in conversation with the tall guy and another lady while I wondered about looking over everything. I was especially interested in a whirly-gig display, but mom had mentioned in a silently understood tone --- NO! So I remember strolling over to the pyramid of cans which began at about my chest height and miraculously terminated as a single can way over my head. Not yet having been schooled in structural analysis, and having a curiosity motivation, I removed only one single can at my chest height. Immediately like an explosion an uncontrolled cascade of cans tumbled to the floor, one of which hit my bare foot causing excruciating pain.

I don't remember what hurt the most, my injured foot or the anxiety attack in my chest. The three grown-ups began to chase down the cans that had rolled into every possible spot but when I picked up one can the tall Guy yelled "Get that dammed kid out of my sight". My mother cried all the way home, but Aunt Fefa threatened to go after the baking powder herself but decided to send one of her older kids.

Politician's Promise

1931 Some loud mouthed guy named Roosevelt said he could solve all our problems since Hoover hadn't put a car in everybodys garage. I didn't think either of them knew how to pour water from their boots even with directions on the heel. "Mickey" mouse was already making money in show business. My bratty brother was becoming a thorn in my side since he was getting all the attention for being the cute little one..I missed my Aunt Hattie who was a million miles away.

My Dad and uncle Francis listened to radio reports about all the things the Roosevelt guy was going to do for every body. Then when they would be home a big argument would sometimes take place between them over Republicans and Democrats. I listned carefully and the best I could figure it out, was that rich people were stingy and poor people were lazy. Dad always said that he liked the rich guys because he never/ever got a job from a poor guy and I wondered what you needed to do to get rich?

Tell you what I can do!

Better Days Ahead

1932 Roosevelt got the President job in November and I didn't vote for him, but he was all for the poor guys like the bunch of guys known as doughboys from WW1 who camped in Washington D C to get their money for saving France. President Hoover owed them, but wouldn't pay and they needed the money pretty bad. An Army guy by the name of McArther beat them up pretty bad and they had to go back home without the money the government owed them. I decided never to get involved in foreign affairs. Seemed to me that foreign countries don't pay good and even rich guys don't either sometimes.

Another guy "Ford" had been making good cars called "T" for poor workers but now was making "A" models which could go 50 MPH. I didn't have one, neither did my Dad since we were poorer than poor. Dad said that rich guys drove Chevrolet's. Some rich guy's baby got kidnapped, Mom wouldn't let me out of her sight, since some radio guy claimed there are Communist or Nazi guys who would like to get little babies to grow up in their country. Dad kept telling her that they were only interested in babies from their own kind. Some guy by the name of Hitler wrote a book that was all about a new race of super people, besides we were too far away from that place to worry. Dad and one of my Uncles used to argue about the Hitler and Rosevelt guys and claimed they and others are all windbags and would be forgotten soon after their next elections.

That Roosevelt guy convienced a lot of people that he could take money away from rich guys and pay poor people to make parks, roads or ditches and hire his friends to oversee these alfabet activities. My Dad was furious about all this and claimed they were all stealing incentive from industrious citizens who could do all these things without his help if he would only get out of the way. I did't worry too much about all these things, but I guess it did make an impression since I became unconfortable around smiling Guys wearing a suit and tie.

Chapter Three:

Dad's Missouri

Prairy Farm

1932 Aunt Hattie and Uncle Harry had left Kansas and bought a prairy farm near Barnett Missouri. We left Illinois and moved in with them, but Dad went on the road working as a day laborer or a shade tree car mechanic. I did'nt go with him but I wished he would have taken my bratty brother so I could have aunt Hattie to myself. Mom and Aunt Hattie didn't get along too good since Mom wasn't exactly the outdoors type and Uncle Harry tried to console her to often. Mom cried a lot and finally after writing to Dad who was staying with his older sister in St. Louis, hitchhicked back to Barnett and got her and my little brother. They left on a cattle truck leaving me behind. They hitched rides to Whitehall Ill where Mom and my brother stayed with a sister again while Dad went back to working at whatever and where ever he could.

Aunt Hattie

Now I suppose it is now time to expose some of Auth Hattie's personality, and why I fell in love with her. She was a very strong minded and tough lady who had married Uncle Harry who was also tough but with out any formal education. They never produced any children and I am certain this is why I became their unfailing devotion right from my beginning.

Uncle Harry had lost most of his hearing at a very young age after having been given away to relatives since he was among the last newborn of about sixteen siblings. He was considered a burden to this new family and as such somewhat mistreated. He developed earaches at a very young age and was subjected to a homespun treatment consisting of hot ashes in his ears,which resulted in partial deafness. His homelessnes brought him to my widowed Grandmothers farm as a young man providing her with farmhelp since my Dad (the only boy) was still very young.

Hattie was one of four older sisters and Harry always mentioned his romantic approach to her as having been "sparking" behind the barn much to Aunt Hattie's chargrin and imberasment. They married shortly after the turn of the century and spent their lives on farming activity. Cooking food and animal husbandry provided Aunt Hattie with a gentilness yet strength to match any man, yet being reserved unless aroused by un- appreciated interferance.

I witnessed a situation involving a government represanitve who came to thier farm requesting full information concerning the crops and plans for the future of these. This was a part of the "New Deal" plan in D.C. to cure the pervasive depresion according to Roosevelt. Aunt Hattie took imeadiate objection to his existance and threatened him with physical corrective action if he ever darkened her doorway again.

She also had strong off-brand religious beliefs more or less self taught mostly concerning civilizations future on this earth. I listened to her tutering Uncle Harry many times and her conviction that he was destined to hell if he didn't change a few things. His most prominant sin was his lack of resistance for joining my Dad or Uncle in a few alcoholic pastimes. He also seemed to need considerable help with spending money wisely since his mathmatical skill was easily misled especially with female encounters.

Barn Pests

1933 Summertime- Un-fortunately the farm barn building near Barnett was infested with hog fleas when my Aunt and Uncle bought it. When we spent time in the barn, the fleas would get on board and nibble away making life miserable. We were obliged to remove all our clothes outside on the porch and pick off the fleas before entering the house. Aunt Hattie learned that if you sprinkled powdered sulfur in your pants and socks the fleas wouldn't get on you. The barn was ridded of the fleas by removing and burning all the old hay, scraping most of the dirt floor and soaking the rest with something (I think it was kerosene). No the barn didn't burn but all the hay was lost.

Homemade Education

I asked Aunt Hattie one time about why there were boundaries in the world and how did anybody know where they were. She found the money to buy a little tin world globe and teach me some geography. The money for that was likely needed elsewhere, and I still have that globe. Home school by lamp light and Aunt Hattie's limited formal education taught me several things especially, to be careful of mealy mouthed politicians. I wasn't sure what they looked like but she said they were almost always dressed in fancy store bought clothes and smiled a lot. They could make rules that everyone had to obey and if you earned any money they could take some of it away from you to spend on

13

things they liked. That Roosevelt guy got all his gang together and started collecting money to put away (in their pockets we thought) to give back to you when you got old. My Aunt Hattie said he was a cheating snake in the grass, since you had to have a number issued by him to get your money back, but that it was only a plan to mark everybody just like it said in the Bible.

All these things kind of bothered me so I decided to just stay on the farm where you could do what you wanted and not be bothered with all those dressed up guys in the big city. I wasen't even 5 years old yet, so getting old was a long time away, anyway Aunt Hattie said that Roosevelt guy would lose his job in a year or two.

Adoption

My aunt Hattie was a fastidious home maker, and would never allow such a thing as field mice in the house. However, I had come upon a nest of half-grown mice under a shock of corn while with my Uncle in the field. I pleaded plaintively to let me keep them in the back room by my bed. These little baby mice were orphans since Trixie dog killed the mother mouse and Uncle Harry kept saying "*that's his job*". Permission granted, but they didn't grow into full size mice because I couldn't get them to drink milk from an eye dropper and Aunt Hattie reasoned with me that they probably missed their mother.

Ten Kid School

This situation took place when I was about 8 years old. My parents were too poor to keep me and my brother at home, so my aunt Hattie and Uncle Harry took the two of us in for the winter. They were farmers on about 80 acres and

had enough garden food canned, meat butchered and cold-packed to take us till Dad could get enough money for us to go home. We were enrolled in the country school with a student body of ten
were seven girls and three boys.

Early springtime finally came around and the three of us boys headed out at a lunchtime break to a little creek that ran behind the school. The bigger boy "named Salters" wanted to catch some little frogs to take back to afternoon class's because he knew his older sister would throw a stinking fit if he placed a frog in just the right spot at just the right time. Besides she had outsmarted him that morning and beat him to the easy "milker" cow before school started. If everything went to his payback plan, she would get in big trouble with the teacher.

I was a year or so younger than him, but I somehow sensed problems with his frog plan and decided that my little brother and I should get in good graces with the teacher to clear us of suspicious involvement. So we went up the creek and found large patches of wild Sweet-Williams and Violets in bloom. We each picked a large handful for the teacher's desk. We didn't wait for the trouble maker to come back and ran back to the school house with what I knew would be our ticket to sweet acceptance.

Instead the teacher raised her hands in aghast and feigned shock that we would destroy mother nature's offering. I suppose this was my first lesson in environmental destruction by mankind (or boy-kind). I was given a punishment of writing a million times (maybe only a hundred) the words "I will not destroy flowers" and since my brother wasn't old enough to write that well he had to carry the drinking water bucket for the next week.

The Salters boy hated to write so he never did turn a frog loose that after noon, but I heard that he forgot to take it out of his pocket and his mother found it some days later. I hoped he had to milk the hard milker for the next month.

Dumb Snake

The hen house where a couple dozen hens and a rooster or two roosted at night was the place where a couple of memorable events took place. The back wall had about dozen wooden boxes where the hens could lay eggs. Aunt Hattie could almost guess how many eggs she could gather each day, but one time she was coming up short for some reason about a week or so. Someone was getting the eggs, and a care full eye failed to discover who the predator might be.

Uncle Harry claimed he had seen a big blacksnake a couple of times slithering around the outside of the building, but that was the only thing out of the ordinary. A black snake was sort of a semi welcome farm creature since they would catch mice, so he was not perceived to be harmful until his tastes changed.

One day the snake had climbed into one of the laying boxes and swallowed a whole egg which created a large lump in his body. This was no big deal since he would eventually curl up tight in a kind of knot and squeeze the egg till it broke inside his stomach. But the snake then decided that one egg was hardly enough so he proceeded to take a shortcut into the adjacent nesting box through a convenient knothole. He discovered another egg and swallowed it whole, which created another large lump in his body. The whole eggs one on each side of the knothole prevented him from crawling through or even backing up, so he was trapped until Aunt Hattie discovered him, presented him to

Uncle Harry & me as jurors and sentenced him to immediate death.

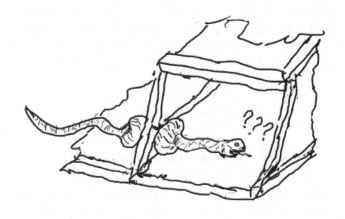

Dumb Rooster

The chickens were always let out of the henhouse in the morning and fed scattered corn on the ground outside. Aunt Hattie had raised some beautiful Rhode Island Red hens and roosters into adulthood. One of the roosters had developed an antagonistic territorial attitude toward his human owners, while protecting his harem of hens. Aunt Hattie was tolerant of his misbehavior since most of the time he would drop his wings and feign an attack just before the corn was tossed to the ground. She mentioned a couple of times *"that rooster better watch his step"* but I don't think the rooster heard her because as time went by he became more aggressive and took a kick in the gullet a few times.

One Sunday he made a drastic mistake and attacked the back side of her legs as she was returning to the house.

He had pecked a little hole and as the drops of blood ran, she grabbed the chicken catcher hook and proceeded to hook his leg while he was engaged in food consumption. He went down on the ground being helplessly caught. In less time than it takes to tell his neck was in Aunt Hattie's hand and his body was being swung over and over her head like a base-ball pitchers wind-up & delivery. The moral of this is *"unless you taste bad, don't attack Aunt Hattie"*.

Dumb Cows

Milking by hand was a daily chore on the farm and the milk was carried to the back room for standing in large crocks a few days. This allowed most of the cream to rise to the top and was skimmed off for sale in town at the cheese factory. Some of the remaining skimmed milk was mixed with ground grain "shorts" bought at the feed store in fancy print cloth sacks. This was hog food and the feed sack material was for dresses, shirts, quilts and underwear. Milk was a very important product and the cows were almost royalty as far as care was concerned.

I was given an old car tire to play with and rolled it almost everywhere I went on the farm. I could play in the pasture where the cows grazed and it didn't take me long to discover that the cows would run like crazy if I rolled my tire at them. This pastime lasted very briefly since my aunt Hattie figured out why the cows wouldn't let their milk down when I entered the barn at milking time. I didn't get in trouble, but I was very gently given a lesson in cow-ology.

Dumb Rabbits

One Saturday when my Aunt & Uncle were in town to sell eggs, pick up shorts for the hogs and staples for the kitchen they discovered that the depot man was paying a nickel each for live wild rabbits. My uncle and I scavenged some old barn boards and built three or four live traps for catching rabbits. For the next month or two I could get as much as twenty-five or thirty cents a week for live rabbits carried to the depot in town on Saturday. I had no idea what this was all about, but was happy as I could be with the money. One Saturday the depot guy quit taking rabbits, I was obliged to turn my five rabbits loose in town and I had already made big plans for that money. This was one of my first lessons in business failure.

We learned that the rabbits were being shipped to Australia to help control some other kind of animal. Approximately 50 years later I learned that the rabbits introduced into Australia became an even greater disaster environmentally, since they had no predatory enemies and proceeded to reproduce exponentially and consume plant life into extinction. Do failures haunt some folks?

Personal Hygiene

The farm near Barnett was equipped with a hand-dug water well a few feet outside the back door to the kitchen porch and an outside toilet at least seventy feet more from the well. This was one of the big decisions to buy that farm according to Aunt Hattie since the toilet would never spoil the well water even though toilet trips were sometimes short notice happenings. She seemed to have early knowledge about environment long before that word came into household use.

Usually every Friday was clothes wash and bath day on the kitchen porch in the summer and bath behind the kitchen wood stove in the winter. Now bathing was an all-out effort consisting of building a fire in the cook stove and placing extra water on the cook top in addition to the reservoir for heating. Dirty clothes were washed first and hung out on the line for drying. Left over wash rinse water was used for bathing grownups first, then us kids if my brother was there. We were now ready for Saturday in town the next day unless of course we got dirty slopping the hogs or any other multitude of messy tasks.

Occasionally the bath was preceded with a haircut by Aunt Hattie using a set of hair clippers that were hand operated by alternately squeezing and releasing the handles to produce a clipping action. Now the big problem with this is, if the handle squeezing is not properly done, the clippers would catch and cause hair pulling. This happened occasionally and while the sting was not particularly painful, I was urged to be tough and not cry baby tears. Being anxious to gain approval and acceptance, I made an all-out effort not to even jump or cry out when this happened. Now my sissified brother would always make a scene and attempt to escape the cruelty of the hair cutting. Consequently, his haircut was mostly done with scissors resulting in a girl looking haircut and of course I couldn't fail to tease him about this. After he went with Mom I didn't have to be as tough to retain my manliness' with Aunt Hattie.

Unwanted Showers

At about 7 years old and living on the prairie farm, I looked forward to Saturday traveling into Eldon Mo. from the farm near Barnett. Aunt Hattie did the road driving of the 1928 Chevrolet since uncle Harry couldn't. Saturday was trading day when eggs were sold and the cream check was collected from the previous week. As mentioned before I was engaged in the business of rabbit trapping and was paid $.05 each at the train depot. We bought hog feed in broadcloth sacks of colorful prints which was made into clothing or quilts and they took up a lot of room in the back.

Uncle Harry chewed tobacco and usually had an empty tomato can on the floor to use as a spittoon in the winter-time when the windows were kept rolled up. However, when the weather was warm Aunt Hattie wouldn't let him keep a filthy can like that in the car and he was required to spit out the window. My back seat was usually filled with cargo of necessities and there was very little room for dodging the shower if things didn't go just right.

Cascading Waterfall

Since living on the farm and having no playmates other than the dog occasionally, it was necessary to find something constructive to do to pass away the long days. I remember gathering many various lengths of firewood logs that were not split yet. I placed them next to each other ends in various stepping heights until I had a towered structure higher than my head. I then gathered tin cans and proceeded to punch a nail hole near the bottom. I would then place the holes in position and fill the top can with water and watch it cascade downward into what I considered a hydraulic miracle. The only problem was, I had created a messy mud hole just outside the back door. Uncle Harry stepped in it and made a mess on the back porch. He got in trouble, but I didn't.

Weather Vane

I spent a goodly amount of time whittling a piece of wood about eight inches long into a propeller shape. When it was finished, Aunt Hattie asked me what I was going to do with it. She had admired the workmanship so much that I felt obligated to make something she would enjoy since I had found out that I would be going back with my parents soon. I decided to complete it into a weather vane that would let them know where the wind was coming from. I completed the project and she helped me mount it atop the smoke house. It worked fine and I received many commendations for the important addition to the farm.

I bought a train ticket several years later back to Barnett as a teenager and was amazed and elated to see my propeller weather vane still working even though the axel hole was worn very much oversize. Good engineering pays off!

Driving Skills

Aunt Hattie was a strong-minded person and was capable of embarrassing a cussing sailor if a situation warranted her opinion of another driver on the road. Not only was she capable of criticizing other driver's expertise, but if a black cat crossed the road in front of her, another route had to be found or even another day for the drive. When none of these options were taken she turned up the worrywart attitude. Uncle Harry would occasionally try to convince her "*don't worry about a cat*" which would nearly always bring down a personality appraisal.

Fence Stretching

The Chevie was used for many things aside transportation and trucking, for instance, one day we were stretching barbed wire fence alongside the long drive out to the County road. All the hedge posts had been set in a straight line of about 700 yards downhill and then up a slight incline to the County road. Aunt Hattie was the engineer of this job and she didn't want to use the horses for stretching barbed wire, so the Chevie was to be used like a tractor. She and I were stationed about mid-way at the bottom of the hill from where the dead-man anchor post was located. Uncle Harry was at the top of the hill with the wire fastened to the car. Since Uncle Harry couldn't hear well, we devised arm waving signals that were to tell him whether to tighten the wire or not as we stapled it to the individual posts in between.

We had completed some three or four posts when the wire became too tight for us to pull down to fit the curvature of the land. Aunt Hattie signaled to him to slack off on the tension, but he had forgotten the signals and proceeded to put the car in gear and drive forward. The extra tension pulled some of the posts out of the ground and Aunt Hattie screamed at me to run for cover in case the barbed wire broke and became a viscous swirling hazard. In the mean-time she was running as fast as I have ever seen anyone and screaming sailors English at the top of her voice at Uncle Harry. Fortunately for him and all of us the Chevie stalled out and all was saved except Uncle Harry's pride.

Chicken House Fire

Rooster butchering was always a lot of work, but it provided delicious meat for visiting company especially when kids and parents made a crowd. Aunt Hattie was an outstanding cook and would make a judgment decision as to how many roosters she would need. Uncle Harry urged her to kill two roosters this time since my Mom and Dad were there. I remember she fussed at him because this meant doing the killing and butchering outside since other food was being made in the kitchen so he agreed to set up scalding and feather plucking outside.

This consisted of building a "campfire" type hot water heater stand made up of three pieces of metal pipe driven into the ground and setting an old wash tub atop these. He gathered kindling and fire wood which was placed under the tub. He decided to put this feather picking operation out back of the henhouse, but had failed to consult Aunt Hattie on the location. He filled the tub with water and lighted the fire in order to get a head start on the rooster butchering. Every-thing was proceeding to his plan until

24

Aunt Hattie came out of the kitchen to check on his hot water set-up.

She immediately disagreed with the location since she had concerns about the possibility of a fire burning the henhouse. The discussion finally ended with acceptance of the location even though it was deemed the most ignorant placement possible. But the water was already hot and moving to another location would entail quite a delay in every- thing. So two roosters were caught, killed and scalded. My Aunt was soon engrossed in feather plucking and butchering. She had directed Uncle Harry to use the hot water for dousing the campfire no longer needed. She returned to the kitchen and an outstanding meal was prepared and served.

We had finished the meal and it was cleanup time when Aunt Hattie returned to the chicken butchering area to gather her knives. Low and behold as she approached the closed gate at the corner of the henhouse she discovered flames licking away in the tall grass along the back wall of the building. Her very high stress personality kicked in and she was faced with making a decision as to whether to run to the front of the building and let the chickens out or to open the gate and run to the back of the building to stomp on the grass fire. She immediately began screaming at the top of her lungs and grabbed the top of a fence post and vaulted over the gate to the back of the building. Still holding the fence post-top she then vaulted back over to the front side to open the door. She was jumping over and back of the gate when my Dad and Uncle Harry heard her screams. They could hardly believe their eyes upon arriving and saw Aunt Hattie vaulting back and forth over the gate. They calmed her and quickly stomped out the grass fire.

This incident was discussed many times especially at family gathering (not in her presence) as to her fence post vaulting ability. There was never any doubt as to her physical strength which could out-work most men, but in a gentleness ability unmatched.

I left the farm with Dad and Mom late that summer. I was disappointed to leave but I am sure the older folks had reasons. Aunt Hattie & Uncle Harry were like Grandparents to me. My wife and children talk about them a lot for they loved all of us.

Chapter Four:

Illinois Again

Another Move

Dad had borrowed a "T" model Ford to transport us and I can remember the journey taking all day and well into the night just to get into St. Louis where we stayed over night with relatives. The biggest problem was because the radiator leaked water so bad that frequent stops had to be made at roadside farms or a creek to refill the radiator and let the engine cool off. Dad had made a temporary fix by adding a little cornmeal to the radiator which would seal the leak holes by swelling up when it became air exposed. A couple of times Dad had to remove a cooked and soaked cornmeal cake at the fill cap since it would make filling with more water impossible. Mom was not impressed with all this since water spills became a problem for me and some of the clothing in the back. The "T" Ford was returned to its owner while we stayed with relatives in St Louis a few days.

Beginning Higher Education

1933, Mom and us two kids moved to Carolton Ill in a rented house. Mom dressed me up in knickerbocker pants and put me in kindergarden. That was a swell place since my teacher was Mrs. Stevenson and she held me on her lap every day until playtime. She thought I was shy and I played that one to the hilt.

Education And Knickerbockers

I don't know for sure but I think we had-to move from Whitehall to Carolton and Dad rented a little house in that town. He was working somewhere else so it was up to Mom to manage family things on her own. She made a lady friend down the street and the two of them decided I should get an education. They took me to the school office and registered me in Kindergarden class even though I was not quite 5 years old yet. I was uncomfortable with all this since there were grown-up people all around and some of the kids were a little playful. The teacher had to guide them when they didn't play what she wanted.and I remember crying since I was shy and on my own in strange surroundings. Luck was with me since my teacher (Mrs Stevenson) let me sit on her lap for several days which consoled me and I have retained her name all my life.

My Mom bought me a pair of pants for Kindergarden school called knicker- bockers that were the fashon rage for school kids. These pants were not long and not short, they came down just below your knees and had tight elastic cufs on the bottom. This design had only one good point which I discovered within the first couple of weeks as follows.

Since not being in school many hours my body was accustomed to being close to a toilet when nature called. I remember walking home after school when the urge struck for a bowel movement. I was walking with a classmate, so to avoid embarasment and knowing that my tight leg Nickerboker pants would keep a secret I simply let nature have her way. The rest of this story needs no explanation.

My bratty brother and me in knickerbockers

Girl Trouble

That little house had a back yard adjoining a yard behind it on the next street. Within the first week or so I met a little girl same age who lived right behind us. We became good friends since she had a little kitten to play with and we spent many summertime hours playing with the kitten in the back yard.

Our house had an outdoor two hole toilet in the yard. One play-day, I needed to use the toilet while after having been playing for sometime. When I opened the door to enter she followed me and said she needed to "go" too and since there was a hole for each of us we just hooked the inside latch and sat beside each other. We enjoyed talking to each other and soon conversation focused on a wasp building a home on the roof overhang outside. She was not real comfortable asout the wasp but I explained that he was not interested in us so we just setteled down to watch that activity.

I remember while sitting there with my feet not quite touching the floor. We both were sort of bumping our heels on the short wall under the seat and simply talking about the wasp. I suppose our mothers had been looking for the two of us for sometime. When they heard our heels bumping the short wall they preceeded to jerk the latched door open and exclaimed shock at the two of us sitting sise by side on the tiolet with the door closed.
We both received physical spankings immeadiatly and some verbal instructions about not ever going to a toilet with any one else, especially a boy or a girl. Never forgot this advice. I didn't know what that was all about but I have avoided going into a toilet with girls ever since.

Eviction

One day we had been evicted when I came home from kindergarden, the big box, table, both beds and other things were out on the sidewalk. But Mom and a lady friend moved our things into the back porch of her friend's house. We stayed with her for a short while until Dad found a small house to rent in the neighboring town of Whitehall. This little house was just across the railroad tracks from the big old tenement building we had lived in earlier.

Crime Doesn't Pay

My Aunt Fefa (pronounced Fee-fee) brought her three kids almost every day and Mom and her cried a lot while we kids played cops and robbers in the yard. One time when it was time for Aunt Fefa to walk back home, Mom had told me to pick up things from the yard and let my cousins get their things together. I searched hard for many minutes for my favorite little toy truck that was a gift from Aunt Hattie. I suspicioned a theft crime was being planned by one of my cousins, but wasn't sure. Not being able to find it, I enlisted help from Mom and Aunt Fefa.

My cousin Junior who was three months older than me remained sitting suspiciously in the dirt play area while every one else searched for my little truck. His mother had asked him several times if he had seen my truck and he had consistently answered in the negative while remaining seated in the dirt. After several minutes, his Mom got suspicious and demanded he get up and help search which he ignored. This time she grabbed him by the arm and pulled him up to expose the toy which he had been sitting on. She borrowed a leather belt from Mom and gave my cousin a lesson in criminal punishment while the rest of looked on. I remember watching gleefully as the dust flew from his back end. We didn't live there very long and soon another move was necessary, but I didn't think the attempted car theft had anything to do with it.

Co-habitation (Dawdy's & Millers)

Dad and Uncle Francis were helping with farm work or digging water wells with Uncle Irvin and digging graves at the cemetary or any other paying job they could locate. I remember Uncle Irvin's tiling spade had been reworked with two openings cut from the spoon body to remove a small amount of wieght each time he scouped earth. His shouvels were hand polished and kept that way in order to make his work a little easier and nobody was allowed to use these tools of a well diggers trade.

Uncle Francis was hand making shoes for us kids by reworking worn out discards of grown-ups. Dad was occasionally driving truck to the stockyards when he could. A four room house came up for rent on Tunison Avenue and we all moved in together. Food was scarce but "relief day" was every other week when staple foods were given out to the needy which was us, I guess.

Dad and my uncles would go to Apple creek outside of town smetimes after dark and "hog" fish. This consisted of wading into holes of water at least waist deep and feel around under tree roots overhanging from the shore. If you could feel a fish, it could be shoved into a toe-sack. This was not a very productive method of obtaining food and it was abandoned after they were nearly caught by land owners a couple of times.

Cousins and Corn

Several incidents took place involving small "corn" town living, my many cousins and other kids. Due to the absence of money and the presence of "New Deal" promises, families of many survived by living together, scrounging necessities and barely paying the landlord.

The Dawdy and Miller families were living together at the end of Tunison Avenue next to the railroad track. The rented house had four rooms with a front and back porch and was surrounded by cornfield. There was a little wood-shed in the back and a corn crib. Uncle Francis had a two-wheel push-cart that would hold about two or three bushels of whatever needed to be hauled home. Winter heat consisted of a wood burning cook stove in the kitchen and an oval shaped sheet metal heating stove (King heater, I think) in the living room. With eight kids to choose from we older boys (the girls never had to work) were required to make several trips a day to the corn shelling elevator building, load the push-cart with corn cobs for heating fuel, empty it into a box on the front porch and go back for more.

Living at the other end of town were other cousins the Fishers (eight of them I think). Some-times we were at the corn elevator at the same time. The Fishers had some mortal enemies known as the Luper kids which numbered too many to count. When it happened that they and we were all at the corn elevator at the same time a major cob-fight war erupted and it didn't end until blood ran or we were all evicted by management.

Now understand being pelted with dry corn-cobs is not too bad as long as you are not being hit in a vulnerable spot. However, my older cousin Pat Fisher had taken a Luper girl shot in the eye a couple of days earlier, and retaliation supreme was required. He prepared at home some weapons of mass destruction consisting of a bucket of cobs that had been soaked in water. These were delivered to the war zone and hidden for a future engagement which took place a couple of days later when all "three cousins bunch (Miller, Fisher & Dawdy)" hung around the elevator long enough for the Luper's to show up. Even though they were out-numbered the Luper's fired the first salvo and General Pat issued immediate "wet cob" retaliation.

Unfortunately, for the Lupers's winter had frozen the cobs solid and the first casualty was a bloody ear. But they returned fire with our own frozen cobs until my cousin Gene took a frozen strike in the mouth. The management evicted us and we were not permitted to gather cobs again without parental accompaniment. The next war was at home with supreme commanders Mom and Mom who enlisted the educational supreme justice's Dad & Dad. I have always wondered if Lupers received any educational instructions like my cousins and I.

Hoop and Hook Snake

Living in the 1930's during the great world depression as a young boy with cousins was sometimes cause for inventing your own fun. The little "corn town" we lived in had a favorite place to play just outside of town. This favorite place was a small patch of wooded area mostly known as "Ross's woods". One of my cousins being the same age as me had a very gullible personality which made him an easy target for made- up stories.

Early one evening just after dark, we had been playing in the woods longer than we were supposed to. I knew we should have gone home an hour or so ago but my gullible cousin was having too much fun and wouldn't leave. Another cousin and I decided that we would scare him with a made-up story we concocted. We started out by asking him if he had seen any snakes in the trees before the sun went down. He informed us that there were no snakes in the trees, but just as he was talking a strange hiss noise caused by two limbs rubbing together in the wind was heard.

This was as great a setting as we could hope for and we informed him that it was undoubtedly a *"Hoop and Hook"* snake. The ploy worked and we proceeded to tell him that the "hoop and hook" snake was probably the most dangerous flesh eater in the world according to our Dad's. It was particularly viscous when breeding season started because it had a great need for warm blood at that time. The male snake was probably the most likely to attack especially if it could drag a young male human to its lair, it became king.

The male snake was about 12 feet long and had a large toothed mouth that could disjoint just like any other snake that could eat frogs. He also had a split tail at the other end and could circle his body into a perfect hoop shape by holding one of the split tails in his mouth. The other split tail was immediately hardened into a hook much like a fishhook with a huge barb. When the snake saw a likely catch from his treetop lookout spot, he would immediately hoop his body and start his roll down the tree trunk directly at his prey.

If you happened to be the target he was able to aim precisely at you and even if you ran a crooked trail, he could steer himself with small hair like legs sort of like the common thousand legged worm that everyone was familiar with. Since he had so many legs he could keep his ground speed up until his hook could be struck into his prey. Your only defense if you were targeted for kill by the hoop & hook snake was to run through water since the snake couldn't swim or breathe under water he would have to give up.

The hiss we had heard was a sure sign of attack and we urged our gullible cousin to run for his life. We convinced him that he was surely the target and go straight for the creek, where he could wade in, wait there while we ran for home. We would be OK and he could come home later.

The warning worked like a charm and we simply headed home and waited until he came in sometime later (wet) to the waist. That was the last time that I can remember him going into Ross's woods especially since he had to shed his clothes out on the porch and suffer the consequences' of his Mom's wrath.

Hoop & Hook snakes are now on endangered lists!

Early Economics

One time a job opportunity came about while living in co-habitation with Aunt Fefa & Uncle Francis in that little corn town. Times were very poor for all of us since between the two families there were eleven people living there, but it was fun playing made-up kid games with the cousins. Dad and Uncle Francis went every day to look for a job except on every other Tuesday, which was "relief" day. On that day they came home with the staples given out by the government to needy families. One Tuesday word was passed around at the relief office that a hiring guy was going to be at the pool hall tomorrow. He would be looking for workers to cut cane for a sorghum mill operation, but in order to get hired you would need to give him $2.00.

Transportation to the job would be in the back of a truck and the job would be good for about a week. The wages would be $3.00 a day but food and lodging would be deducted at $1.00 a day when payday arrived. We were all jubilant that evening at the prospect of our dads getting a job to bring home some money, however there was the problem of raising the $4.00 job cost. Everybody was requested to produce every penny of savings or rent money that was available. We were able to gather $3.00, but my uncle Francis said he could borrow the last dollar from the guy who owned the pool hall.

The job lasted four days with the last two being in continuous rain, so the truck was loaded after supper with workers and returned to town. An accounting session between the two families erupted with some heated discussion. The final count was net earnings for the four days of labor for two men with families was $16.00. With the family treasure of $3.00 & the borrowed $1.00, my Dad and Uncle cleared $6.00 each for four days' work. This was my first recollection of the power, exasperation and meaning of economics. The new president elected had promised a "New Deal" for everyone, but it wasn't until the next decade that either of our families recognized any significant improvement in economics.

Aunt Fefa Tough

Whitehall was probably no more than a thousand strong and was mostly surrounded with corn crops. The rented house was at the very end of town, off a back street in the middle of corn on one side and a railroad on the other. Aside from four adults there were seven kids of various ages from about twelve down. I was probably about six or seven and I had a boy cousin Junior three months older than me. He had two younger sisters Peggy and Ellie and an older sister, Betty. Located in the back yard was an old woodshed, an out-door toilet and a corn crib. The empty corn crib was about eight feet square and the walls were made of slats about 2 or 3 inches apart. There was loose wood on the floor and a sheet tin roof. The purpose of this building was to fill it with ears of corn for storage and drying until shelling or feeding.

Hot summertime in Whitehall could be a boring time especially if you are young and full of energy. My cousin Junior and I had spent the entire morning cracking black walnuts and picking the meats out for my Aunt and my Mother for some kind of a cake. It was Tuesday and our Dads were in town getting relief food, so there would be flour and sugar for that. Holding a walnut between your thumb and forefinger while smacking it with a hammer is not only tedious but dangerous too if you miss since the girls didn't know how to hammer. We had emptied what seemed like bushels of cracked shells of their meats before it finally satisfied the cook's requirements, so we were ready for some boy type entertainment.

The three girls had been excused from work detail (which was always the case) and had been allowed to occupy the empty corn crib all morning while we boys were assigned walnut cracking duty. They had gathered blocks of wood, pieces of tin, various rags and whatever it took for them to create a corn cob baby-doll playhouse complete with mud pies and table settings. My cousin and I had smashed our fingers several times while cracking walnuts and were more than ready to quit and find something we could play with.

We attempted to share the corn crib doll playhouse a couple of times but were rejected by the screaming protests of the girls, backed up by Mom and Aunt Fefa. After the second or third attempt was made, we were instructed to come in the house and sit on a bench across the room from the windows, so we couldn't even see the girls.

The day was miserably hot by this time and we were consigned to that bench for what must have been hours. We squirmed and fidgeted and were antagonized by an occasional girl cousin peeking in the window with a spiteful tongue out.

When we protested the length of time the punishment was taking, the punishment team decided to hear our plea and asked what we intended to do if we were excused. Not having any specific plan in mind we simply began to complain that there was nothing to do. So, we were re-assigned to the bench until we could come up with an acceptable plan for ourselves. We began to whine and squirm thinking that we could obtain freedom by putting mental irritation on our captors and asking over and over *"what can we do"*. This worked for another few minutes until my Aunt Fefa lost her patience and yelled at us

"GET OUT OF HERE AND GO PLAY WITH YOUR PEE-PEE'S." **WE RAN.**

Having obtained freedom, we decided to fix those girls. They had abandoned the corn crib playhouse by now and were probably buttering up our Dad's who were now home. We entered the abandoned corn crib playhouse with the full intention of total destruction in mind and rebuild it as a fort, but although the girls weren't playing in it anymore they caught us and reported us to the authorities. We were threatened with more "bench sitting" punishment if we didn't leave the girls things alone. So, we vacated immediately, if not sooner and vowed to get even. We were instructed to sit on the outside water well platform and think about our activities.

We began pumping water out on the ground thinking of creating something out of mud that could be of use, but were instructed to stop wasting water and sit down somewhere. While sitting on the water pump foundation together, drinking lots of water and squeezing mud between our barefoot toes, we formulated a revenge plan.

When every-one else was busy in the house, my cousin Junior and I climbed up the back side of the corn crib and proceeded to PEE between the slats on as much of the play household items as we could hit. NO! We didn't get caught since the girls had abandoned the playhouse until several days later. But: Just think, if caught, Aunt Fefa might have destroyed our weapons.

Junior & I are not in the picture (multi-family decision) but here are the good ones.
Back row (L-R) Aunt Fefa & Francis Dawdy-My Dad-Aunt Dona & Goldie Fisher
Next row Brother Donald &-Cousins-Ellie-Betty-Peggy-& the little ones didn't bother us.

Dick Tracey Apprentices

Telephone poles located on some of the most important streets were important electric power supplies for the community populace. They supported wires for electric services to those who were lucky enough to afford the luxury of lights or listening to entertaining radio programs. In addition to the electric services these poles supported telephone wires which provided communications for business, emergencies and important gossiping.

My cousins and I made a very important discovery that provided information of untold wisdom and importance concerning secrets not available to anyone else. We found out that if you put your ear to the damp side of a telephone pole, you could hear conversation that was being made between persons if they were on the phone at the time you were listening. We discussed this among ourselves and decided that we should listen for clues concerning criminal acts or plans and maybe divulge this to the town Constable if it involved bank robberies or cattle thefts.

Since (Gene) one of my cousins lived on a street that had telephone poles near his house, he volunteered to listen in on conversations every morning. My other cousin (Junior) and I had no telephone lines running past our house, so we had to leave our house and find listening poles some distance away. Our search met with some unexpected discoveries starting with our ears being blackened with fresh tar from new poles soaked in preserving pitch. We didn't realize this until our Moms insisted on knowing how in the world we got tar on our ears. We managed to keep our secret discovery away from them by claiming to hide behind a pole while playing cop and detective. Mom used a little kerosene on a small piece of cloth and warned us about the tar on our clothes.

Continuing research effort on our part produced more valuable knowledge in that all telephone poles do not produce the same quality of conversational information. First-off we discovered old poles were the best and there seemed to be better sides of the pole to get the best sound reception. Also, there was definitely some better telephone conversations than others, both quality and quantity. Some women conversationalists had nothing of interest except how they were feeling and what their kids were doing. But occasionally we would find out that Mr. Somebody better get his fence fixed or he may never see his cow again. My cousin Gene found out that the movie theater in town was showing some movies that were downright shameful.

We applied our newfound informational source for at least a Month before finally abandoning it for lack of Constable worthy information and beside we were told by one of our older cousins that lightning always struck telephone poles even on sunshine days.

Grown-ups didn't have much to talk about, but future kids learned how!

Junior and I knew some town secrets

42

Trains and Railroad Tracks

While living at the Tunison Avenue rented house, being adjacent the railroad track was both good and bad depending on how you interacted with it. It was a source of coal fuel for the winter stove if all in the family took toe sacks in hand for coal picking and walked the railroad track curves. The best pickings were after a fully loaded coal car went by and some of the coal lumps spilled out. Dad & Uncle Francis swore there was a fireman that missed the boiler door sometimes if we kids would stand by the tracks with toe sacks in hand.

However the summer time offered a little different challenge for us boys, especially when the apple tree had green apples that could be launched from the end of a sharp stick as the train passed by. The railroad people never caught us, but my aunt Fefa did. My cousin and I were instructed to cut an apple switch, which she used with corrective instructions

Boy's Big Bang

The first half of the 1930s was sometimes filled with adventure for my two nearly same age cousins and myself. Because we lived adjacent the railroad track and were sometimes enlisted to retrieve coal chunks for home fire use we also were allowed to wander along it for fun. The railroad had maintenance crews that patrolled the tracks from time to time and we were absolutely not allowed to be on railroad property when they were around. Now these guys rode on a four wheeled "herdie-girdy" cart fitted with a stand-up handle that when pumped back and forth propelled them along on the track. When they reached a place that

43

needed maintenance, the cart could be moved off the track if a freight train needed to pass their work area.

The work crews place would sometimes be some distance away, so a cookie shaped noise making "BANG" device on the track would warn them of an approaching train. This little flat explosive devise had a narrow strip of lead about six inches long embedded in it. The intended use of the lead was for wrapping it around the rail to hold it in place until a train would run over it making a "BANG" noise warning.

One time the three of us found one of these "BANG" cookie noise makers laying on the gravel bed beside the rail since the little lead strip had failed to hold it in place. Now we had to make a decision as to whether to replace it on the rail or leave it where it was on the gravel bed. Our combined logic was "don't put it back on the rail because the work crew might set it off and blow-off a "herdie-girdy" wheel, so the only reasonable thing to do was take it home and hide it along with our other treasures".

Decision time passed slowly and worries mounted considerably with the possibilities of adult discovery? Then there was the possibility of a Constable search crew discovery? Maybe we could just fasten it to the track close to the house and let the next freight explode it, but what if that caused the train to stop and investigate? Maybe we could just throw it in the water reservoir, but then what if it poisoned the town drinking water? Finally, it was decided to return it to the railroad track where it came from. My cousin just a little older than me put on bib-overalls late in the afternoon, so he could put the "BANG" cookie in a pocket to avoid discovery since this devise had taken on a scary discovery avoidance importance. We departed for a stroll on the track with instructions not to be gone very long since supper time was coming. Our house was the last house on the track before entering cornfield countryside so we decided to go that way to avoid any nosey eyes.

After traveling some distance, we decided to get rid of our explosive treasure since we came upon a pile of four new wood ties and first thought about placing the "BANG" cookie on the top. My cousins devised a plan to put the cookie under a top tie. The three of us then stood another tie on end balancing it vertical over the cookie tie. The plan was to see if the cookie would detonate if we dropped the vertical tie on it.-- IT DID!

However, we were stunned by the "BANG" to the point that our ears rang for the next couple of hours.

Hygiene Lesson

The following incident has been told in our family many times and since it took place long before I was old enough to witness, I will relay it as told to me.

When my cousin Junior was some-where between the ages of 3 and 4. He had an intense interest in playing with what-ever was before him, in fact a concentration that he many times would not stop long enough to poop in the toilet. He would simply use his pants and suffer the consequences when he was odiously discovered. Several whippings had yielded little, if any results.

One day he entered my Aunt Fefa's kitchen smelling strongly like an occurrence had taken place. Narration as I've been told is as follows:

Aunt Fefa: *"JUNIOR! HAVE YOU POOPED IN YOUR PANTS?"*

Junior: *"No Mom"*

Aunt Fefa: As she grabbed his arm and began lowering his overalls.

"I'M LOOKING AN IF YOU DID I'M GOING TO RUB YOUR NOSE IN IT."

Junior: squirming and crying since he knew his guilt. *"No-no-no"*

Aunt Fefa unknown to Junior had been preparing pumpkin for a pie. She scooped an appropriate amount in one hand while holding him with the other and instructed him to look what she had found in his pants.

Junior: Not realizing that what he was seeing was pumpkin in Aunt Fefa's hand began screaming a protest as she generously rubbed his face with pumpkin.

Aunt Fefa: *"NOW YOU SIT IN THAT CHAIR UNTIL I TELL YOU TO GET UP WHICH MAY BE TOMORROW."*

I am told that Junior never failed to use the toilet from that day on, at least, I can verify that he never used his pants when we were together in later years.

Aunt Dona's (pronounced Do-nees) Free Spirit

At the other end of the little corn town was an Aunt Dona and Uncle Goldie's house furnished with eight kids. Being at the edge of town they had a milk cow, some chickens and usually a butcher hog or two. Depression days of the early thirties being tough times for many folks so any one who had a job was extremely lucky. I suppose Uncle Goldie was one of those since he had a job firing the kilns at a clay tile producing company. His job was long hours, seven days a week and I seldom saw him, except occasionally at meal time.

The frame house was basically four rooms and most of the kids slept on cots or the floor. The kitchen had a long table where Uncle Goldie sat at one end and the kid's all sat on benches along the sides, except the two oldest boys who always scrambled with each other to sit at the other end from

Uncle Goldie since he was prone to "back handing" kids that got out of line.

I don't ever remember my Aunt Dona or the oldest girl sitting at the table, and table manners mostly consisted of who could outreach or out scramble any others. I was always treated kindly by Aunt Dona or the oldest girl (Doris) with biscuit, buttermilk and a piece of chicken delivered directly to my plate. In later years, I determined that the oldest girl was not well liked by her step-father Goldie. The rest of the kids were on their own and "survival of the fittest" seemed to be the household rule. I loved my Aunt Dona since she was mostly a free spirit person and pretty much let the kids get into and out of trouble on their own.

Swimming at the "Res"

Aunt Dona's house being the last house on the street at the opposite end of town from Aunt Fefa's was almost like total freedom since my Mom and Aunt Fefa kept much closer tabs on us than the Fisher household. I suppose the reason was because there were more boys than girls and Aunt Dona being more free spirited than her sisters. Anyway, a fraction of a mile farther out of town from the Fisher's was a clay tile processing company that transported clay for forming and curing into drain tile shapes. A narrow-gauge rail road track and what we referred to as "the dinkey train" traveled slowly back & forth from the clay pits to the kilns. The town-water reservoir was a small lake out by the clay pits which afforded the best swimming hole you can imagine. The distance to the swimming place was about three miles, so my cousins and I would hang around the dinkey train track and catch a ride out and back to the "res". This worked pretty well until one time my Uncle Goldie caught us hitching a ride. He was furious that evening, but Aunt Dona just said *"BOY, I WISH I HAD BEEN WITH THEM"*

1934 War Games

Living among many family's worth of boys in that small corn town during the 1930's world depression gave cause for inventive competition of rubber-gun development. Prior to WW-2, automobile tires were lined with nearly pure rubber inner tubes which had a good amount of elasticity. Tires on vehicles were driven until the treads and cords wore completely thru which eventually caused a blowout rendering the inner-tube damaged beyond repair. My older cousins seemed to have access to some of these inner-tubes which they cut into strips of varying widths for use on home-made rubber-guns.

If we younger boys worked off some of the older boy's chores, we could be paid with some rubber strips, so that we could build personal rubber-gun weapons. A gun was usually made from a small piece of corn crib slat about a foot or so long. A square cut nail was driven partway into one edge close to the end. A full circle of rubber was stretched around the entire slat-barrel and a flat trigger stick was inserted under the slat- end rubber circle. This provided a pinching place for a strip of rubber which would serve as a bullet when stretched over the length of the slat barrel.

Several weapon development programs were pursued, always with the end design to produce more range for the strip bullet and more kill-power in case of a war. The usual gun design was single shot and the basic thought was to have more than one gun available if you needed two. However, one of my older cousins came up with an over-and-under design that consisted of two rubber strip bullets.

We played war among ourselves for several days which were generally conducted in a "hide and shoot" method. After we tired of playing war among ourselves we decided that it would be fun to challenge the "Luper" kids for a war game. They being mortal neighborhood enemies, a more meaningful weapon needed to be developed, so one of the older boys created a weapon that would leave evidence of a kill hit. He drilled a small hole in the end of one of his slat guns and placed a couple of ripe elder-berries in the hole. A rubber strip bullet was then stretched over the berries and loaded into the pinch trigger. The berries were squashed under the rubber strip bullet and he now had what was later identified as tracer bullets in WW2. The loading of this weapon was a bit messy but a hit was even more satisfying, especially if it was a head shot.

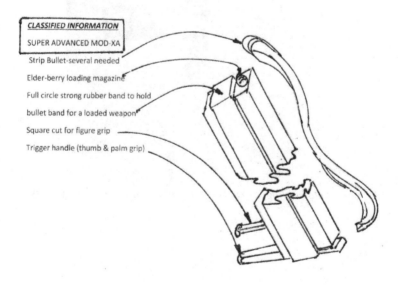

Use of this weapon was outlawed by one of our mothers since the elderberry stains were objectionable as far as they were concerned, but we all hoped that the Luper mother was even less demanding. This peace council demand was likely a good thing since we were considering an elderberry weapon of mass destruction consisting of a sling shot to launch multiple berries from a special pouch. Peaceful co-existence shrouded the neighborhood for a few days at least until the stains washed away.

Picture of me holding my rubber gun pointing down for safety's sake.

Marble Yard

Summertime days at aunt Dona's house was fun filled in several ways, since we were a group (three related families) of four boy cousins nearly the same age plus one older one by about 5 years.

The front yard had a very large Maple tree that shaded probably 50 feet of the area. Little grass could grow since there were several other smaller children and also kids from across the street that seemed to congregate there. Summer had been hot and dry for some time and the yard was dedicated to a daily game of marbles mostly for anyone in the neighborhood that possessed gambling material. My cousin (Junior) and I each had a small bag of marbles at home and when we went to play with our (Fisher) cousins we would put a few in our pocket expecting to enlarge our hoard.

Another family in town (Lupers) had more kids than any-one else but we generally avoided them due to their rowdiness and reputation. One day three Luper girls and one boy showed up and it was decided that we would let a couple of them into the game since they were sporting some real "keeper" marbles. Everything went fine for the first hour or so, and my winnings were growing along with my cousin Gene, but my cousin Junior was losing big-time. One of the Luper girls (who we really didn't want in the game but was coerced with accusations of being afraid of losing to a girl) was using a "steeley" shooter. Due to the extra size and weight of her shooter she was sometimes able to claim two or three marbles each shot, since that steely had a tendency to car-rom off onto our baiter marbles.

My cousin Junior began to cry when his wealth had been reduced down to just his shooter which was a prize cat-eye. The Luper girl offered to trade him five marbles for his cat-eye shooter, but when the trade was done by the closed hand method he put up a howl that could be heard everywhere. My cousin Gene approached him inquiring what the trouble was, and Junior showed him the traded marbles which were mostly chippers undoubtedly gained as a result of her "steeley" damaging them. Now Gene was short tempered and proceeded to punch the Luper girl in the belly since she refused to relinquish her ill-gotten gain. That was a big mistake since she was bigger than him and she immediately wrestled him to the ground while pummeling him with clenched fists and slowly squeezing the breath out of his midsection between her locked legs. Junior entered the fracas at this time by grabbing her around the neck in what he hoped was a choke hold.

In the mean-time her younger brother was pocketing as many marbles as he could from the unfinished game and I challenged him by jerking his pocket open and spilling the contents on the dirt yard, He in turn arm-locked my neck attempting to wrestle me to the ground, but I was too tall for him. The fight was pretty well under way when my Aunt Dona exited the house armed with a witches' broom and dispersed the free-for-all with some well-placed shots. The Lupers departed while uttering threats of lifelong retaliation promises.

All four of us cousins were directed by Aunt Dona to wash each other's back while standing in the wash-day rinse water tub after wrestling on the dusty marble yard. All marble gambling was abolished until further notice, but I wound up with the Luper "steeley" which, I failed to divulge for fear of aunt Dona's broom but cousin Junior made me share some of my loot since he had lost a lot of his.

Dirt Town

Due to the closure of our marble gambling area after the recent riot, one of my older cousins at the Fishers suggested that we turn the area into a miniature town. He (Jackie) was about five years older than the rest of us and usually avoided us kids, but this time he offered management for the project, if we would do all the work. We were verily impressed with the idea and began preliminary work which consisted of considerable grass removal, all by hand while sitting or kneeling. Since no rain had fallen for several weeks the earth soon turned to powder as we began making roads and bridges over an area probably twenty feet square. There were four of us boys working and one older one supervising. We worked diligently all day long and had created a kid's model dirt town complete with stick houses, corn cob cars and airplanes and even a skyscraper from cardboard.

That night a severe thunderstorm passed thru and deluged the dirt town with several inches of water. The next morning I and my fisher cousin, Gene were awakened at daybreak by Uncle Goldie"s screaming about the mess in the front yard and the pile of fresh mud and grass right in front of the porch steps. My older Fisher cousins (Jackie and Pat) claimed no responsibility for the flood devastated town even though they had participated, consequently Gene and I were assigned to yard reconstruction. Junior my other cousin escaped since he had gone home the evening before.
I suppose that's why I have always been a little cautious about "community building"; cleaning up your mess ain't fun if you make a mistake.

Hitler Is Dead (as told to me later in life)

During the early 1940's WW2 was in full force and our country was pumped with propaganda to support our war effort. Aunt Dona was in the process of raising a young pig for butchering or marketing depending on which would produce the most benefit when the hog reached maturity. She had named the pig "Hitler" in keeping with the sentiments of our country at the time. My youngest Fisher cousin (Leonard) was likely about 4 or 5 at that time and had been playing in the back yard most of the morning. Lunch time came at which time buttermilk and biscuits were put on the table. The young cousin casually made a statement at the table *"Mom, I killed Hitler"* and my Aunt simply said (in keeping with every one's general attitude) *"That's good son"*. Nothing more was thought about the statement for an hour or two until Aunt Dona decided to water her pig. She discovered her young Hitler pig dead from a brick that Leonard had dispatched to rid the world of a villain. Aunt Dona was heard to say over and over as they ate the young piglet *"O, My God, there goes my new teeth"*.

Bum's Hollow

My cousins and I could visit with our Taylor grandparents who lived at the other end of town but when we wanted to go to my Fisher cousin's house from there it was necessary to cross the railroad tracks. Since my Grandpa being a retired preacher, I think the railroad bums knew a place to get a handout and marked his house someway. There was a section near the town dump and a curve in the railroad track known as "bum's hollow" which I passed through many times going from Grandma's to my Fisher family cousins. Many times there were several bums sleeping under the trees smoking, talking, singing and even shaving from a kettle of campfire water. This curve in the tracks was a place where the train slowed down enough for the bums to get on or off I am sure. We were never bothered by anyone, but we had been warned not to waste any time getting through.

Grandma's Table

I can only remember a few things about my Grandma Taylor who was always wearing an apron and seemed to always be cooking something. Her kitchen table was always covered with a cloth in the middle with jellies and biscuits under it. She made grape jelly from the back-yard grapes growing over the path out back. Any time I visited her she would insist that I have some jelly biscuits and a glass of milk.

Preacher Grampa Taylor being retired occupied his front porch most of the time that I can remember. He was always playing solitaire with a deck of cards and a story about one time when one of his parishioners questioned him about the "sins of the card deck" he retorted *"I've always told you, do as I say and not as I do".*

Young Boy's Air-Show Dream

During the so called repairing days of the (1930s) great world depression, our family was still nearly destitute. However, a few things were progressing in other parts of the populace of which I had very little knowledge, such as the emerging growth of aircraft and travel for the privileged. Summertime was mostly boring in our little corn-town but occasionally a light bi-wing airplane would fly over-head which always caused a considerable stir among all of my boy cousins. A plane would usually fly from the south and if it were anywhere near our town we would chase as fast as we could run all the way to the other end of town. Of, course we would always arrive at the north-end other cousins house long after the plane was out of sight, but most times the airplane event was discussed as to who it might be, or where it may have come from. Our imaginations would most-times override actualities and if the plane had been flying low we were sure it had taken off just the other side of the cornfield.

One day out of the blue sky, flying just over the treetops a plane skimmed our town from one end to the other then made a sharp full turnaround and began dropping leaflets over the four-block long business area. The whole town was outside watching as the plane made another full turnaround and flew really low and loud making a sharp climb skyward and was soon out of sight. A scramble to retrieve one or more of the leaflets ensued and I was lucky enough to get one that had landed in a puddle at the bottom of a ditch. Two of my cousins were given an ice cream cone (single dip) for their leaflets, but I kept mine since it was wet anyway. One cousin let me have a lick of ice cream since he wanted his mom to see my leaflet and he could plant an idea.

The leaflet was advertising an upcoming circus in the next town north of us in two weeks. Pictured at the top of the page a bi-wing airplane and an ad stating rides would be given after the first day in which an air show was to take place. The air show consisted of a daredevil that would climb out of the cockpit onto the wing while his partner buzzed the field. Also pictured were some trapeze ladies (with hardly, no clothes on), a bearded lady and a fortune teller. There would be a Merry-go-round, a Ferris wheel,

Shooting gallery and many other attractions like elephants and lions.

Also, the tallest man in the world (Robert Wadlow) 8"11" was going to be at a shoe store to meet people (this was free) and there were free ice cream cones for the first 10 kids under 8 years old to bring their Dad or Mom into the clothing store. There was some other advertising about ordering a new car any color you wanted, black, green or even maroon and delivery charges could be forgiven if you picked it up somewhere in a town called Detroit.

I could hardly wait to get home to show Mom the paper and ask if we could go. Mom just looked at me and said *"We'll see"* and my heart skipped a beat since I was pretty sure that meant we would NOT be going, but I would look at the precious paper and dream anyway. The show was in the next town of about fifteen miles and we had no way to get there until I suggested that maybe Uncle Irvin could take us on his ice delivery truck.

Two weeks crept by and my cousins and I had many discussions about the air show event that we dreamed of attending. But the day before the show Uncle Irvin's truck burned out a clutch and no transportation was available. Mom would only say "*some-times dreams are only dreams*" but a young boy's heavy heart and airplane fascination would be hard to forget.

Chapter Five:

Missouri Farm Living

Mom's sisters and brother in Whitehall Ill. couldn't take us in anymore especially since Dad was out of town somewhere working. So we had to move elsewhere which meant back to Missouri where the Miller kinsmen lived.

Borrowed Cow

My Dad and Mom rented an old farmhouse outside Eldon Mo. Dad had negotiated a deal with the farmer-owner that we could live in the old house as long as he would milk several cows for him morning and night. The dairy farm was about ½ mile down the road from where we lived and just beyond that farm was another dairy farm owned by an Uncle Albert to my Dad. Dad was able to obtain an odd job here and there from time to time to bring in a few dollars for household expenses. We had no car, but Dad was usually able to borrow something when we needed to go into town. This was usually and old flat-bed truck which needed to be worked on regularly, especially tire repairs. Money was very scarce so garden vegetables and an occasional squirrel kept us living the life of the depression days that all the politicians were going to change for the better.

One day my younger brother (Donald) and I had walked with Dad over to Uncle Albert's dairy farm to meet with some guy who was thinking of hiring Dad to help re-roof his barn. We were all out next to the big milking barn and my brother (about 5 yrs old) had wandered into the feed

59

lot where several "milker" cows were. Generally, milk cows are rather docile animals; however, one particularly large black & white Holstein apparently took a dislike to the little boy wandering into her territory. She lowered her head and began to charge toward my brother. Dad caught a glimpse of this and quickly scaled the gate boards into the lot yelling at the top of his voice at the lumbering cow, however the cow managed to knock my brother backward and stepped on the side of his chest as she veered away from my screaming Dad.

Dad scooped up my brother and began consoling him about his torn shirt and the bleeding abrasions along his side. Now we were in no position to afford a doctor so it was decided that medical attention would have to come from whatever was available. Uncle Albert produced some salve that he claimed would stop the oozing blood and hurry the healing process. They applied the salve and wrapped his little chest in washed torn-up feed sack material pinned with safety pins. My brother screamed un-mercifully and continuously. Uncle Albert volunteered to drive him & I home to our Mother while Dad stayed back to get the roofing job.

Upon arriving home, Mom and my Grandma Miller "set-in" on Uncle Albert about how the boy got hurt and why was he screaming about the medical application. It was determined that the salve used was a homemade mixture of lard and turpentine usually used on cow's scratched udders when necessary. Warm bathing water and an abundance of motherly lap attention finally ceased the sissy's squawking, and I still believe the turpentine poultice cured his scratches sooner than all the attention he was able to command. As I recall he refused to wear a shirt for several days just so every-one would be unable to ignore his mortal wound. I was never able to get that kind of attention even with near fatal wounds suffered many times in my childhood days. But anyway, on with the rest of this story since my brother and I had many encounters that showed plainly that he was always the favorite.

Smart Cow "Satan's Sister"

That was the first encounter with that cow for our family, but our association grew as follows. It seems that Uncle Albert got the word that our family was in pretty dire need of food. So, he volunteered to loan that same cow to us for the milk she was producing.

It was spring time and we had several acres of skimpy timbered pasture and a small shed where she could be housed for milking time and overnight protection. Dad attempted to walk her home on a short rope without a halter and soon discovered that she had a stubborn streak that was barely tolerable. He found out that she could not be led and could only be driven, so he procured a long stick held in one hand and the loose end of the rope in the other hand. As long as the cow reasoned that she was going in the direction that she wanted to go progress was made. However, if she decided to veer off course dad would take corrective action with the long stick.

The mile or so journey from the dairy farm to our house was a turning point in my Dad's life since he vowed not to let a (#%^>*) cow rule him, especially since we needed the milk. The big lumbering black and white Holstein was given a formal name that day of "Satan's Sister". Dad borrowed a halter soon after her arrival so he could at least tie her up for milking and she detested this handy human handle. Stubbornness was likely the best part of her personality and following are some of her more predominant characteristics and cunning.

She was a quantity milk producer low in quality since little cream would be realized from a considerable amount of milk. Obtaining the milk was a daunting chore due to her stubbornness since she would invariably "hold-up" her milk. When you had finally begun to obtain a partial bucket, she would dance into it (spilling it over) and knocking you over at the same time if possible. Dad soon learned to tether her tightly to the side wall of the shed since it had never intended to be a milking facility and therefore had no "stall" for milking. He also learned to use some borrowed "kickers" which are simply a couple of sheet metal hook shapes fastened to each other with an adjustable length of chain. The intended use for this devise is to place one hook to a hock protrusion on a back leg, bring the other hook and chain around the front of both back legs and hook it just above the other hock protrusion, at roughly udder height. The use of kickers is to prevent a cow from kicking with a hind foot since both legs are tethered together with the kicker.

It didn't take Satan's Sister long to find out that she could kick with both back legs "jackass style". Now this was extremely dangerous if you happened to be behind her and I think it was very satisfying to her if she could strike the bucket of milk on the return of both feet. Since our shed type milking facility was small she managed to kick a fair sized hole in an outside wall using her jackass kick and knowing full well that she had been tethered to close to the wall behind her. We learned that when she was thinking of making a jackass kick, she would sort of crouch down a little on her front legs and lean forward. We learned to tether her head up higher to prevent the crouching. You didn't dare sit on a milking stool or never-never use both hands to milk, for as soon as she determined both hands were busy, she would urinate or lean into you or both.

The milking process was tedious at best and impossible to accomplish without a test of wits between Satan's Sister, my Dad and usually me since my little brother wouldn't come near her. Now Dad always claimed this cow would intentionally seek out wild onions or any other foul tasting pasture just so she could deliver a Satan's Sister flavored milk as often as possible. Finding this cow in the evening for milking time was a challenge since she could find the best place to hide in the woods and would stand in one spot with a full udder dripping on the ground rather than submit to milking. She hated the human handle (halter) so much so that she would find a place in the woods to hang the halter and break it. She seemed to know that she was fully in control when this occurred and knew full well that we would be obliged to spend considerable time locating the halter most of the time hooked on a fence post.

We finally got one that she couldn't break and Dad located a cowbell to attach to the halter. She soon learned that milking time was coming up soon and would stop moving her head so as to silence the bell. A couple of times she found just the right forked tree trunk and was able to snap the bell off the halter. We had trouble finding the bell of course and dad swore that she would intentionally move to another spot behind some blackberry bushes too separate her from the crime scene.

Smart Dog

Dad was busy milking for our landlord in the evenings and since Satan's Sister was devious I was given the chore of locating her and put her in the shed. I had a dog that was a true prey-drive type animal and I decided to put his talent to good use in handling Satan's Sister. I would manage to get the cow sort of running from the pasture to the shed by whacking her with a stick and then I would encourage old "Socks" to keep her moving by biting her on the back legs. Socks got kicked a couple of times before he decided to attack higher up from the heels and feet. He learned that he could leap up and grab on to her tail at a point just where it came out of her butt. This worked very well since Satan's Sister couldn't kick him as he hung on while she lumbered toward the shed.

I was pretty proud of myself for solving a vexing problem of cattle handling but after a week or so my dad discovered the wounded tail where Socks had been hanging on to Satan's Sister. He questioned me and explained that not only was I teaching my dog something that could get him into big trouble, but also the loaned cow was a financial obligation if she became sick or dead at my hands. So, Sock's had to be untrained (punished) for something I had taught him and I soon decided that Satan's Sister was not worth the cheap milk that she produced. Dad agreed with me and decided to return her to Uncle Albert using the excuse that our fences were not good enough to hold her.

I managed to get a good bit of satisfaction before her return since I was given the opportunity to apply the lard and turpentine to her butt several days to hide the dog bites. I have always felt that if she could have talked I would have heard some of the same kind squealing that my sissy brother had done when he was "turpentine-d".

Blinded Stop

One summer day while living in this old farmhouse my younger brother challenged me to a game of "blind-man's bluff". There were several old fashioned Bridal Wreath bushes and large trees all around the big yard which provided many places for a youngster to hideout. Mom and my Grandma Miller who was living with us at that time were busy hand washing clothes outside on the porch near the well. So we enlisted my Grandma to be the timer and score keeper. One player was to blindfold himself while the other player was to hide somewhere within the confines of the yard. A voice signal from the hidden player was the signal for Grandma to begin timing for the blindfolded player to then remove the blindfold and begin searching. If the hidden player could return back to Grandma before being discovered a point was won.

Now my brother was prone to cheating by changing hiding places behind my back after the start. So, I decided that if he could cheat it wouldn't be wrong if I countered his tactic by peeking from under the blindfold. We had selected a starting place around the corner from where grandma was busy with the wash. We signaled for a start and my brother ran around the next corner, but I had carefully slipped one little peeking hole under the blindfold. When he ran around the corner, I decided to run after him in order to watch where his hiding place was going to be. The blind fold slipped down into place as I began to run and I collided with the corner of a brick chimney. I fell backward as the stars and darkness engulfed me. The next thing I recall was warm liquid on my face and the taste of blood as my head began to throb. Of course, I then screamed and Mom and Grandma came to my rescue. I have often wondered if that incident has had any lasting effects on my mental capabilities, cheating is dangerous.

Sharecropper

Being urged to give up the rented farm for "milking duty" we began living at Dad's Aunt Ollie's farm outside

Eldon Mo. in a little cabin by the barn as a sharecropping family. Dad became acquainted with a neighbor farmer down the road from us. It was late June and this neighbor farmer was complaining to my Dad about the poor stand of corn his seeds had produced. He had about 30 or so acres of rocky soil planted and said he would like to get someone too re-plant the voids with new seed he had bought. My Dad told him that he had two good sons that could be trusted to replant where ever missing plants were discovered if the man would pay them. The farmer jumped on the offer, but failed to make any kind of monetary commitment. This was discussed at home during the middle of the week and my Dad said we could do the work on the next Saturday and not to worry about the money since he felt the farmer was a fair man and would pay us well if we worked hard.

The next Saturday, my younger brother and I reported to the farmer at about 5:30 am. He gave each of us a seed bag with a shoulder strap and a "pike" pole. He warned us not to plant anything outside of the row so the cultivator could plow without cutting corn later on. We understood the rules and began the laborious task in the bright sunny morning. I remember talking between ourselves about the big money we were sure to get. We didn't finish that day so returned the next day to finish, however the sun had blistered our backs the day before and mom had caked our backs with baking soda poultices and issued heavy shirts with sleeves. We finished just after noon but the farmer was in church so we didn't get paid.

The following week was filled with anticipation, but no word from the farmer, so my Dad visited him on Friday evening to find out about our pay. I will never forget the astonished look on my parents face when Dad returned with our .50 cents each which was thought to be fair for a couple of share-cropper kids.

Wrongfully Accused

This incident happened one very hot spring day when I was about 8 years old living on my dad's Aunt Ollie Jones's farm as sharecroppers. It was a Saturday morning and the night before had been spent cutting two bushels of seed potatoes into seed sprouts for planting the next day. I had assumed the planting was going to be done by my dad, but something of great importance came up that required my parents to go into town. My dad woke me up early, and informed me that my younger brother and I were to plant and cover the seed potato eyes.

Two thirds of the garden harvest, was to be Aunt Ollies and I must mention that she was a miserable landlord to my folks and especially to my brother and I. She could hardly tolerate the two of us and we were instructed never to go anywhere near the big white Victorian house she and her old-maid daughter lived in. The garden at the side of the house was bordered and shielded from site by a grape arbor. My brother and I toiled very hard to plant the nearly four bushels of cuttings as the morning sun and humidity punished us with-out mercy. But we were determined to get the job done so we could go swimming in the creek in the back pasture.

We finished the job and decided to take a little rest under the shady grape arbor. I can still remember the cool breeze drying the sweat on my body, however we were totally unaware that peering eyes were watching from the house. We heard dad in the borrowed car (cousin Opal's) come into the drive way on the other side of the house, but remained in our cool shady spot. We also heard the heated conversation over the usage of the car and most of all the accusation that those two boys *"HAVEN'T EVEN TOUCHED THE POTATOES"*. My dad being hot tempered stormed around the corner of the house with belt in hand and proceeded to punish both of us for being lazy and laying around in the shade. Finally, he heard our protests and looked on the other side of the grape arbor at the empty potato seed baskets. One of the few times I remember seeing my dad shed a tear as he instructed us to go to our cabin. I remember his seething personality as he slammed the back door on his way into the big white house.

I also remember several times that summer powdering the potato plants for bug control with **<u>arsenic</u>** and how we were evicted from the premises later that year with no share of the potato crop and I don't think a share of anything else. But then maybe I really didn't know everything except Aunt Ollie and Opal were not very much fun to be around and that maybe the arsenic didn't have an effect. I have since learned that Arsenic causes tingling of the extremities, I wonder if that included Aunt Ollie's tongue?

Heritage Sharpshooter

My Dad's (Miller) side of the family tree was filled with some wild and wooly characters from the early days of the pioneers in the mid-west part of the United States. In approximately the year of 1935, Dad introduced me to an old man whom he called "Uncle" twice removed at a Sunday afternoon family gathering at Aunt Ollie's. Several of the young and old men-folk had gathered out behind the barn and were engaged in some mild betting concerning their target shooting ability with the rifle kept in the barn for whatever it may be needed. A firewood log had been moved into place and some tin cans were lined up atop it for targets. I remember a considerable amount of hassling each other about wasting 22 cal. bullets when some-one failed to hit a can.

After a box of cartridges had been almost used up, the old Uncle my Dad had introduced me too spoke up and asked one of the men to go to the house and get his pistol and holster behind the kitchen door for him. While strapping his holster and pistol to his waist he began to chastise the rifle shooters for using still targets and a long gun. He goaded some of them into placing a bet that he could toss a tomato can in the air and keep it in the air until his six-shooter was empty.

Some of the guys smiled at each other knowingly and some of the others laughed and bet something. The old Uncle selected a quart size tomato can and walked several steps away from the barn, hesitated a moment after drawing his pistol. He then tossed the can straight up in the air, carefully took aim just as the can hesitated for its return trip and fired a shot almost straight up. I will never forget the impression this made on me watching the can suddenly change direction upward for what seemed nearly as high as the crest of the barn roof. The old Uncle took a step or two to reposition him-self just under the can as it again hesitated for its return to earth. Four more careful aims and shots were fired and each time the can danced upward. The bettors were stunned and looked at each other in disbelief while some of the knowing smilingly advised them against betting the other man's game in the future and informed them he was probably saving the last shot in case the bets didn't get paid.

Ambushed

Dad told me the story about this same old "Uncle" twice removed and how he had been required to survive many times in his life. Once, when he was a young man, he and his brother using the family horse and buggy, spent a

Saturday night in town gambling at a local tavern. He had won a considerable amount of money from the other gamblers which had included his brother. Late in the night his brother declared that he was broke and intended to take the buggy and go home since losing all his money. He left the tavern but the "Uncle" remained for some time, stating he would come home on a borrowed horse. A few miles between the tavern and home was a railroad crossing on the road and as the "Uncle's" brother approached this he devised a plan to retrieve his lost gambling money.

Knowing that his brother would be coming across this same route he decided to fake a hi-way robbery for his brother to see. Using railroad crossings for bush-whacking was a fairly common hi-way robber's tactic in those days especially the Jesse James gang. He carefully turned the buggy on its side tethering the horse's legs just outside the drawbars. He then lay down on his stomach under the buggy with a club hidden under him. He calculated that when his brother discovered him, he would busy himself with righting the buggy off his body which would provide him with an opportunity to club him from behind. His plan to regain his lost gambling money could easily be blamed on robbers especially if his brother was unconscious and had been drinking enough before going home.

The plan failed when the "Uncle" caught a glimpse of the club descending on his head, at which time he withdrew his pistol and was tempted to dispatch his brother. On second thought, he proceeded to pistol whip him and leave him unconscious by the roadside. The entire incident was blamed on road robbers and it was many years later that the true facts were disclosed.

This family gathering was shortly before we were made to leave the farm. Dad always felt that Aunt Ollie's son from out of town had something to do with our being forced to leave the farm since crops were mostly in by now.

First Love

Dad was share cropping and I had found a friend on the next farm. My best friend Harry Lee Ray and I would wander almost at will around the nearby farm pastures and roads. One summer day we were walking with our Captain Marvel pedometers when we came to the back yard of a neighbor. As we came around the corner of the woodshed a lady was hanging clothes up to dry on the back-yard clothes lines. She was startled by our invasion and quickly demanded to know where we thought we were going. As my buddy stammered an explanation I noticed the most beautiful girl standing just behind her mother with a half (Mona Lisa) smile as she listened to the questions and answers between my friend and the lady.

It was love at first sight, but it was not until school started a few weeks later that I found out her name, Annette. My best friend was infatuated with her best friend and we would waste hours-planning romance. We decided that the girls would be greatly impressed if we could give them a memento ring or jewelry. Since we had no-way of obtaining rings we decided that we could make them each a bracelet. Our bracelets were original creations made by chewing short pieces of bare copper magnet wire into small pea size wads and then stringing them together to form a bracelet. We chewed copper for at least a week during school hours while admiring our intended girl friends in a one-room schoolhouse. Finally, our opportunity came to lavish the girls with bracelets at a Saturday afternoon matinee free movie show in town. We didn't know they were in the theatre until we went up in the balcony. I first sat down in the row behind Annette but when she invited me to sit beside her if her girlfriend would move back with my buddy.

After many minutes of stupefying silence as a reel change was being made, and since there was nothing on the screen I casually presented her with the bracelet I had been carrying for several days. She was very appreciative and I was sure that this would be my lifetime girl since she let me twist the copper band together around her beautiful wrist. After two more reel-change's we exited the theatre and was met by her mom at which time she proudly showed the bracelet.

Her Mom was not very receptive and made some kind of remark about a "bummy" sharecropper. The next couple of months were spent in a small one room country school, but I never saw that bracelet again and Annette filled the school days with careful avoidance. Everything probably worked out the best since our family was made to leave Aunt Ollie's farm late in the fall due to a disagreement about crop farming and we moved into town.

Female Wrath

We rented an old building in Eldon for a little while after being removed from Dad's Aunt Ollie farm just before Christmas. We lived 2nd house from the corner and our back yard ran all the way to the alley. There was a house around the corner in which lived a girl in my grade at school. I had hardly noticed her since girls were kind of hard to get along with and especially since they always had a Mom watching their every move. Her name was Eileen and her back yard was fenced with solid boards about four or five feet high.

It was my job each night to split firewood for the cook-stove in the kitchen. The woodlot where I did my splitting work was about a foot lower than her yard at the fence line. She began to hang on her fence each evening and many times made little comments to me about my work, especially when I would miss my mark with the axe. After several evenings of poking fun at me, I lost my patience and told her to shut up and tend to her own knitting.

She disappeared in the house and I didn't see her in the back yard for several evenings until one evening she came out and offered me a piece of cake and said she wanted to be my friend. I was flattered and ate the cake immediately as she continued to apply friends talk. I had finished my wood splitting for the evening and was preparing to go in the house when she suggested that she give me a kiss since we were friends. She was taller than me and since her yard was higher than mine, I had no way to get close enough to kiss. So I selected a big block of un-split wood, moved it over to the board fence, climbed on top of it and gave her a goodnight friendship kiss over the top of a solid board fence.

Next day in school at recess she approached me accompanied by two boys. She commanded them to hold me by the arms while she slapped me on the jaw. She had told the boys that I had forced her to kiss me the evening before. I never did understand her motives but, I was determined to get even so I gathered some dry cockleburs from the weeds along the alley. Eileen had long hair well below her shoulders and my opportunity to get even came just a few days after the slap. I had been carrying the cockleburs in an old Vicks bottle and as she was passing me on the way home I launched three or four burrs with perfect marksmanship onto her hair while following behind a step or two in silence. She didn't feel a thing and I thoroughly enjoyed listening to her screaming as her mother was trying to remove the burrs from her hair on their back porch.

Flying Machine Fascination

While town-living in Eldon I became infatuated with a purely novice attempt at creating a flying machine. Development of this project was taking place several blocks away from where we were living. My introduction to this project came one evening when an almost deafening sound came from around the corner street. The sound was a roar of exhaust combined with yelling of encouragement over whatever was taking place. This lasted about two or three minutes and then silence. My Mom and a couple of other neighbor ladies gathered to discuss the incident as I listened in. One lady seemed to have inside knowledge which consisted of an irritated opinion about some young guys being a genuine nuisance to the neighborhood since they were trying to develop a flying machine.

The fascination with aircraft potential was a worldwide competition for being creative in anything involving airplanes and mankind or even womankind or in my case boy-kind. My curiosity about the noisy, neighborhood disturbing-guys simply intensified after I learned that they were trying to develop a flying automobile. The project was apparently under-funded since the work underway consisted of an early model Ford car they had modified by adding a sloping nose made from a baggage trunk lid attached to the front bumper to create an air foil effect. They had removed all seating and doors from the body and had attached wings on each side and a homemade tail fin and rudder arrangement. All glass windows had been removed since I now think they suspected an emergency landing.

The noise I had first heard was simply a premature development test run to determine ground speed that could be expected for a successful takeoff at some later time in development. These tests were shut-down by the Town Constable but considerable conversation between me and some other boys my age continued as to the potential of this much-needed invention. I didn't live in town very much longer since another family move was made, but I never forgot the fascination and dreams of my own as to the possibilities of a flying machine for every-day use by the common man.

Another Fascination

The above incidents were not necessarily my only encounter with the female species at that age. I had been fortunate enough to attend a movie "Heidi" where I saw the most beautiful girl that was ever born, and she was the most intelligent person of my age that you could imagine. I vowed to run away from home just as soon as I could and go to Hollywood California where she lived. She was the star of that show and I found out that she was the same age as me, so I knew there would be no problem claiming her when I got there. My love lasted for quite a while and I knew she probably wouldn't marry me right away at least until I could get a job. Finally, my love faded since I was never able to gather bus fare for the trip.

Later in life, I found out she married someone else and changed her name from Shirley Temple. But I was already in love and married to Betty by that time. I heard that she became a big important person in politics and got herself a job as an Ambassador for our country. Lady luck was probably with me after all, since I love my country and am sure I wouldn't like living in some other country with Shirley. We moved back to Illinois again after spending a little time with St Louis relatives.

Chapter Six:

Illinois here we come again

Sharecropping' Over-With

1935 Roosevelt and his wise men were burning hogs and telling farmers not to plant crops so the prices would go up according to Aunt Hattie. We had moved back to Ill and were renting a house across the street from the corn elevator building. Roosevelt had a "New Deal" where you could work for the CCC or WPA or PWA. I didn't work for any of these and my aunt Hattie couldn't sell crops or hogs acording to her letters. My Uncle Francis Dowdy had been taken to jail for failure to pay rent by the local constable, but he got out after a night or two. Dad and Uncle Francis spent a lot of time in the pool hall finding out how to work for the Government or any body that needed help. Share cropping had not been to good unless you owned the land, so Dad quit it.

Lady Luck

1935 Dad lucked out by taking a job in Carrolton Ill at the CCC camp in the motor pool where he was paid $28.00 in cash each Month and got excess messhall food when available plus family access to the camp doctor. We rented a house up the road from the camp about a ¼ mile. While walking home from school one day, mother nature called upon me with a certain urgency. I was wearing another pair of knickerbocker pants that was thought to be representative of our national hero (Lindberg) of the time. My thought was "keep walking since the tight fit at my lower legs will hold things" until I got home. It didn't work out that way and by the time I got home I was a rejectable sight to behold. Mom was less than kind with me since she was sure that I knew better and was capable of recognising bodily messages of importance. She made me climb into the wash water tub on the back porch waiting to be emptied. I was really embarresed to be bathing in plain sight of the neighbors who lived in our back yard. Mom was pregnant with another bratty brother but I suppose this was a convienent clean-up fix for that situation and I vowed never to bathe in public again.

The Flower Thief 1935

One day a lady who lived just the other side of the CCC camp visited my mom and during the visit she promised my mom a bouquet of flowers if I went home with her to bring them back. This is exactly what I did, and when the lady picked what she considered a bouquet I was sent home with a measly offering for mom. Mom was pleased, and I decided since the lady had such a large collection in her garden untouched, a few more would not be missed. I proceeded to return to the garden and select a few more for mom. After about two more flowers the lady came to the door and shouted at me *"please don't pick any more of the flowers"*.

This upset me considerably to be caught red-handed in an "in progress" robbery as a 7-year-old flower thief. I immediately began running from the crime scene. I was running (thinking, surely the lady was right behind) intending to escape into Moms arms. Since the escape route was adjacent the CCC camp, my Dad intercepted me. His full 5'6" hulk reached over the fence and pulled me up to his eye level. The stolen flowers dropped to the ground. He unmercifully tried and convicted a professional flower thief practically at the crime scene. Since he was on duty at the motor pool he quickly passed sentence to be administered after work at home. I was sent on my way to await my punishment. Death for the next 5 hours could have been much sweeter.

The Little Man 1935

The terrain around our rented house on the outskirts of Carrolton was mostly flat farmland with drainage ditches on all the gravel roads. Another family of trailer house renters lived in our back yard and they had a son who was probably the biggest show-off anywhere. He was so proficient at cartwheels in the yard that he could do like five full turns. One day when my Dad and his Dad were sitting on our back porch this smart-aleck kid did his cartwheel act. Not about to let him gather all the approval nods and smiles, I made a full speed running approach and a perfect entry into what was to be at least a six turnover cartwheels. All was going well until about the fourth turnover of perfect form, even though I was beginning to lose directional control due to dizziness. Suddenly the drainage ditch swallowed me and excruciating pain ensued in my right knee. Looking down I saw a gashed knee and what must have been gallons of blood squirting. Looking up I saw my Dad picking me up and the smirking face of the kid next door. My Dad reassuringly said to me *"don't cry son, be a man"* so I didn't.

He decided that I needed medical attention and began carrying me down the road to the CCC camp. We went into the dispensary and Dad sat me on a table with a white cloth on it. It looked just like one of the tables in the mess hall except it had a white cloth on it. A man in a white coat came into the room and pinched at the huge cut in my knee. He looked at my dad and said *"looks like he will live, but he is going to need some stitches"*. *"Don't have any anesthesia, what do you think?"* My Dad said *"he's a man ain't you son? **he** won't cry, **will** you son?"*. A big curved needle and thread was produced and as I sat on the edge of the table while the horse doctor for the camp sewed three large stitches right in front of my eyes. I didn't cry but my Dad did, because I saw him turn his head away just in time for a big tear to drip from his nose. We went back home and the next couple of hours were hero heaven as the men bragged about the "little man" in front of the women and the smart-aleck kid.

Fights 1935

The CCC camp was a behive of activity that provided many incidents to be discussed in the evening. The camp was inhabited by mostly young men, both married and single. It was sort of run by officers like an army where there is an officer in charge of the camp who made all the rules. One of the rules concerning argument settling was if you had an argument, it could never be settled in the field. Every Saturday night an outdoor boxing ring was set up for those that needed to settle differences. It was a bare fist, no brass knucks or knives fight to the finish and no outside help. The camp doctor was there to attend to missing teeth or earbites. An audience was permitted and, one time over my Mom's objection I went with my Dad to watch a friend of his beat a smart ass guy he didn't like. I never fought there and neither did my Dad for that matter. Dad explained to me that this was not a good way to settle differences, but don't ever back away from a fight if you think you are right.

Revenge

Another time a serious incident took place in the field that probably cost Roosevelt some money. A young truck driver was fooling around with a farmers daughter near a drainage ditch work site. The farmer caught him and threatened him with a shotgun if he didn't stay away from his house. The young truck driver decided to get even, so he drove his CCC truck into the front porch of the farmers house. The last we knew of the young truck driver was that he was in the brig and scheduled to be moved to a place called Leavenworth. *"Punishment for the poor can be serious"* Dad said.

Fox and Hounds

While living in Carrolton, sometimes I was invited to go fox hunting at night with my Dad and the neighbor man from the back yard. The neighbor had a couple of fox hounds and a car (dogs were named Lead & Boss and I don't know what the car was named except it was called a coupe with only one seat). When we loaded up to go hunting, I had to sit in the middle and old Lead dog had to sit on my lap. Boy was he stinky but very friendly. Old Boss was crabby and he was always put in the trunk. Upon arrival late at night at the hunting site, the dogs were turned out to begin hunting and we would make a campfire. This was the best part of the night since Dad taught me how to cook bacon strips on a stick (from the CCC camp kitchen), listen for the howel of the dogs as they chased a fox and other nighttime sounds of the woods.

After several hours of listning to dogs and the grown up men talk I sort of dreaded the time to go home if the dogs came in. Old Lead who had to sit on my lap was always soaking wet and panting like crazy in my face. If I was lucky the dogs wouldn't come in and the men would have to leave their coats on the ground for the rest of the night for the dogs to lay on and be picked up next morning.

Run Faster

Another quick story about those dogs that were kept tied up behind the neighbor's house trailer. Old Lead was a friendly dog and some-times we were allowed to let him loose to play with, but old Boss was crabby and kept tied on a chain. My brother couldn't resist the temptation of teasing old Boss just out of chain length reach. One day while old Boss was sound asleep on the ground my brother decided to tickle him on the nose with a long weed. Old Boss woke up in a hurry and made a leap forward as my brother presented his backside for a quick retreat. My brother had miss-judged several things and old Boss got him on his seat of education. When my Dad got home that evening the other side of his seat of education got another lesson for teasing the dog.

In 1936, I think the CCC camp was closed by the government and that Roosevelt guy was very popular with the grownups still waiting for a "new deal". Aunt Hattie and Dad both said he was done but he got back in office anyway, and our family was still plagued with no money. He had started a government thing where everybody was given a secret identification number that was never to be used by anyone except the government for money you would get when you got old. Aunt Hattie claimed knowledge from the bible that was the beginning of a masterful plan to mark every-one in the world for subjugation to the devil. My brother and I were sent to live with Aunt Hattie on the farm early in the year while Mom and my youngest brother stayed in Ill and my Dad went out on the countryside looking for work.

Chapter Seven:

Back in MO with Aunt Hattie

Shared Boots

I attended that one-room "ten kid" school (7 girls & 3 boys) during the trying times of the great world depression before WW2. Likely, since I was living with my Aunt and Uncle very little money, if any, was being forwarded for my keep. When the winter came, my brother and I were taken to school in the horse drawn box wagon. Blisters were on my feet since I had outgrown my only pair of shoes, so my younger brother got them until enough money showed up for another pair. My aunt rode to the school and I am almost sure that she explained to the teacher the shoe situation. The school was heated with firewood and all students were expected to help keep the fire going. Since I had no shoes, Aunt Hattie had put several socks on my feet and wrapped feed sacks over that so that my feet would fit into Uncle Harry's rubber work boots. This lasted for a couple of weeks, until a new pair of shoes was bought out of cream check money. The only good part of all this was that the teacher didn't expect me to get wood for the fire since I was sort of clumsy in that emergency foot-ware.

Food for Thought

School year 1937/38- I have always liked the taste of whole grains and have eaten my share during my lifetime. I think I know the reason, it's because when I was very young and attending school, my Uncle Harry would encourage me to put a handful of thrashed wheat from the grain shed in my pocket and chew on it until it became a lump of dough in my mouth. This taste would make the thought processes and hunger pangs more bearable as I was confined to a seat among the other nine kids in our country school. I was the only kid in my grade and the teacher required me to busy myself with written or reading assignments while she taught the other grades. So I studied and chewed.

Uncle Harry never attended school, so I don't know how he knew this would be of value in school. His knowledge was mostly practical learned and he had another use for soaked wheat. He loved to "trot-line" fish for carp and he would always make up a batch of soaked wheat pressed into little ball for baiting the hooks. He said *"ifn it'el help catch a carp it'el, help ketch some larn'in"*.

You can see (in the doorway) Aunt Hattie teasing him for thinking like a child.

86

Wet Bed

Carp fishing provided food and pastime for my Dad and Uncle Harry if they could talk Aunt Hattie into doing the chores while we went overnight fishing on the Osage River just below the Bagnel dam. This was trot line fishing consisted of tying a line to a tree and placing the other end weighted with a big rock out in the water. Dad always had to drive the Chevie and he had renewed an acquaintance back on the County road who owned a wood "john" boat that he would loan to us.

They would load the boat into a box wagon and tie the long tongue to the car bumper and tow the boat about a mile to the river. This was always fun because Dad let me ride in the boat, Aunt Hattie never found out about this and I never told. We would then stretch a hay rope all the way across the river between trees on each side. This was used to keep the boat from drifting downstream as we fastened baited hooks onto the trotline. We were then set for a night of trot line fishing.

One time, I had insisted on sleeping on a folding army cot near the water's edge while the men mostly stayed in the car between trot line runs. I loved to listen to the gurgle of the water pouring over stones or exposed tree roots at the water's edge. The stream was fairly fast moving just below the dam and Uncle Harry always claimed that the Carp fish were better eating since the fast-moving water "cleaned" them up. Dad would just smile and agree. I remember being awakened abruptly in the middle of the night with water pouring into the side of my cot. As I rolled out of bed into water above my knees, I yelled for Dad. Unfortunately, Bagnel dam management had opened the locks and the water level jumped some four or five feet in a matter of minutes. We lost the bedding and cot to the current as well as the argument with Aunt Hattie next day for allowing me to sleep by the water's edge.

Hogs

Uncle Harry was one of the best hog raising farmers according to most stories told in the neighborhood. He was also known for his expertise in castrating boar hogs for neighbors. One time he and Aunt Hattie had saved the life of a little piglet who happened to be the runt of a litter. This little pig was so small that he got pinned behind the mother sow and the wall while all the rest of the litter was nursing. Uncle Harry found him almost dead when he was feeding and the sow stood up for food. Uncle Harry picked up the nearly lifeless body and put him in his jacket pocket while finishing his chores. It was cold weather and likely the warm pocket revived him somewhat. Uncle Harry brought the little pig into the house and Aunt Hattie began feeding him warm milk on a soaked dish cloth held between two figures.

She was determined to save him till the next day since they were scheduled to go into town where she could buy a nursing nipple. The continuous care and his new home in the kitchen firewood box behind the stove apparently agreed with him. He grew in size, soon became a house hold pet with his own name "Oinker". He earned the privilege of free run of the farm, but really didn't stray very far from Aunt Hattie's foot-steps. Uncle Harry played with him and taught him to fetch a stick, and he seemed to love being poked with a walking cane if he got in front of you. His reaction to being poked was to turn around, grab the cane and run away a few steps and wait for someone to retrieve the cane. This was a high-energy activity and the only way to stop the play was too simply go away and leave him with the cane in his mouth.

After he grew into a full-fledged shoat and on into young hog status, his continuous presence in the house became more and more disrupting. He was very polite and accommodating before entering the house since Aunt Hattie had insisted that Uncle Harry wipe off his feet before entering. "Oinker" grew into a full-fledged hog and a reluctant decision to ship him off to the market had to be made. A livestock truck arrived to pick up hogs for the market. "Oinker" had been put in a holding pen with the rest of the hogs. The hogs were being herded into the loading chute by the driver, however when he poked "Oinker" he lost his cane and was unable to retrieve it. The loading process was stopped because of all this. Finally, the exasperated driver went to the house where Aunt Hattie and Uncle Harry waited since they couldn't bear to watch "Oinker" load up.

After considerable conversation Uncle Harry simply went down to the loading pen and said to "Oinker", *"C'mon follow me"* as he simply walked up the loading chute into the truck bed. Aunt Hattie always said that it is always a mistake to name a farm animal if its destiny is food.

Suspicious Thinking

My aunt Hattie was considered by some as eccentric, esoteric and religious fanatical to a degree. She just wanted to work hard, accumulate enough money to pay-off the bank and mind her own business. She had a sixth-grade education and read the Bible to help interpret life meanings and cautions.

A battery-operated radio was kept on a kitchen shelf and it was occasionally turned on in the morning to listen to the live-stock price report since Uncle Harry occasionally shipped hogs to the market. News reports occasionally disclosed political reports about a guy who came into power by promising to retake land that rightfully belonged to Germany. Some of the countries still spoke the German language, but considered them-selves separate from Germany and wanted no part of a book he had wrote called *Mein Kampf* a sort of Bible for his party called Nazis.

Now this character named Hitler insisted on expansion for a greater Germany. The more Aunt Hattie heard, the more she insisted that we better keep our eyes on him, because he represented a method of power which could happen to us. She was very opinionated and suspicious of many in our own government who seemed to be attempting to tell farmers not to raise crops, steal gold and hire loafers to build things nobody needed.

I listened to some of these ramblings, but couldn't quite fathom how a Hitler guy half way around the world could possibly cause trouble in the middle of our country. Uncle Harry who was, uneducated, nearly deaf and toothless would just sit in his rocking chair and shake his head in agreement, then when Aunt Hattie tired of preaching he would acknowledge by saying something like "*Ol Pearl* (a work horse) *kicked the dog ystday*".

Now I'm not going to say, listening to these homespun opinions had much lasting effect on my ability to measure circumstances, however some of my adult life decisions have been tailored after him or her.

Chapter Eight:

Lucky St. Charles MO Here We Are

Teen Age "Here I Come"

I have just read another article about the plight of Mexican people attempting to enter the United States in hope of obtaining a better life. The struggles of these people bring back memories of a time in my-life that is similar to the plight of many, right here in the United States. Following is a real and actual experience for what it is worth as I count my blessings.

My father was the only boy in a family of three older sisters and two older half- sisters. His father was killed when my Dad was only 9 years old. As a result, he was pitied and spoiled as a young man to the point of never being given responsibility. His youthful time was caught up in alcohol and fun which ill prepared him for the rest of his life.

Advance now into his adult life of marriage and family of 3 young children (myself, two younger brothers). The year 1938 was filled with many enticing promises and government sponsored economic recovery programs designed to end a 10-year depression. Lack of employment in these years was very much akin to the present-day situation in Mexico and there is a possibility of similar times for us ahead.

After having drifted and dragged our family over a three-state area, my Dad heard that he could get a laborer job in St. Charles Mo. working the Mississippi river with the

Army Corps. Engineers. (Another time-failed Gov. program). This wasn't exactly the case and after leaving Mom and us boys with relatives he joined two other hopeful hitchhikers to St. Charles Mo. It was late in the fall and the river program was grinding to a halt since ice flows in the winter presented project problems in previous years.

No money, no job, no home & no friends (other than the 2 hitchhikers), my Dad found himself in another tough spot. Dad was somewhat mechanical and managed to make a small amount of money occasionally working on old cars. One job he related to me was for a wealthy businessman who had a Packard automobile in his garage. He told my dad and one of his friends they could live in his garage if they would keep his car washed and waxed. Having had a job a couple of years previous in the motor pool for the CCC's my dad knew a little secret method learned there concerning vehicle appearance. He simply washed the car in kerosene in the evening and wiped it next morning, which gave it a brilliant waxed shine.

While the housing situation was a bargain, the accommodations turned very poor as the winter came on. The garage, an old building behind the business at Kingshiway & Clay streets had a dirt floor, pretty well oil soaked and a sliding door rotted out at the bottom. Sleeping accommodations consisted of some auto seat cushions donated by a local auto shop in exchange for some work.

The winter dragged on & on but, making acquaintances at one of the local bars, dad heard that a canning factory would be looking to hire some people when the season started. Lady luck was with him and the canning factory offered him a truck-driving job before the season started. Aunt Hattie had arranged for me to ride with a hog trucker headed for St. Louis. I stayed a few days with another Aunt in St. Louis until Dad could pick me up. The factory foreman and dad became bar-buddies. Dad and I were allowed to take the truck to Illinois to gather his family and possessions. I remember my cousins were disappointed at my leaving, but one Uncle mentioned something about riddance. I couldn't quite figure that out since I always had a good time at his house playing & working with the many cousins we had there.

We moved into some upstairs rooms, on the corner of South Main & Booneslick streets over a neighbor-hood grocery store. The canning factory was right across the street and life was good since eventually my mom got a job sorting tomatoes. With labor money coming in, my Dad started spending more time with his foreman bar-buddy which always seemed to be important to him. One evening, Dad put Mom and us three kids in the tomato factory truck to show where he had lived all winter in the garage. I shall never forget the impression that made on me looking at the rotted-out door and knowing there had been no heat or lights all winter while I was living comfortably with relatives. This is the kind of work desire that most all of us in our wealthy country has had no recognition for, in the last 65 or so years. My Dad was a hard worker, but he was also a hard player. Our Mexican labor invaders are motivated by need to provide as was my Dad in 1939

First Bicycle

In the summer of 1939 I was almost 12 years old. Dad had been hired to drive truck for a tomato-canning factory. Since I was the oldest child, I was expected to watch over my two brothers while my Mom worked sorting tomatoes at the same factory. Dad gave me $2.00 a week for doing my job. I had declared earlier that I wanted to earn money to buy a bicycle that was for sale down the street.

93

The bike was an old one that a kid by the name of Cameron Blair had put together from parts obtained from a bicycle repair shop up on 2nd street by the Missouri River Bridge. It didn't look too good and it had no front fender, but it had longhorn handlebars and leather fringe on the back of the seat. Cameron was a pretty good talker and he was 15 years old I think. He told me that the bike was going to be bought by a rich kid that he didn't like for $16 but he would rather see me have it for $15. I told him that I was working and saving up for the bike and he promised to hold it for me.

There was an old couple across the street who said they would pay me to cut grass for them so I jumped at the chance to add to my savings. The lawn mower was a manpowered reel type with a handle that came about shoulder high on me and I think it must have weighed 100 lbs. Fortunately, the lawn was not much bigger than two houses and it edged a creek that I could cool off in. I could cut the lawn in about three hours and they gave me .50 cents each time.

I finally accumulated the $15 and was all set to go buy the bike when Dad told me to wait till he could go with me. I really didn't need his help but I dared not talk to Cameron without my Dad. It was nearly a week later before Dad could find time to go with me, and by that time, I had almost $18. We went down the street one evening and Dad refused to let me buy the bike because it didn't have a front fender. Cameron was mad and said he thought only a sissy-boy needed a fender to keep his feet out of the spokes.

I was heartbroken and felt like giving up my job. Mom didn't have to work the next day and Dad insisted that I ride with him on his trucking route. He told me to bring my money with me and maybe we could find a fender for the bike somewhere. We drove across the river into Wellston and stopped at a Firestone store. I was amazed to see at least

94

a dozen new bicycles all shining and bright. Dad asked me if I liked any of them and my eyes fell on the most beautiful blue and white "Firestone Cruiser" bike you could ever see. It had a tank with a horn button on the side, front and back fenders, a light on the front fender, a luggage carrier on the back, white wall balloon tires and matching handle-grips. The price was $40 but Dad said he would advance my next week's wages and match my half if I liked the bike better than Cameron's.

I rode my new bike all up and down South Main Street the next week and got in trouble for not watching little brothers as much as I was supposed to. I could make it as far south as the water-works and north to Clay Street in about 8 minutes if I didn't put my butt on the seat. That was probably the fastest bike in town and even that rich kid didn't have one as good as mine. I didn't dare ride the new bike down Boonslick road because that was where Cameron lived.

About two glorious weeks had gone by when one day my mom didn't have to work and my Dad wanted me to ride truck with him. I could stay with the truck while he delivered partial orders in some stores. My younger brother was home and decided to ride my bike that day even though he had been instructed not to touch that bicycle. But he proceeded to push the bike down Boonslick to 3rd street. He was not big enough to reach the pedals, but he could coast down-hill. He proceeded to push the bike up the steep third street hill then climb on and coast down. When he coasted to the bottom of the hill the street ended. He flew across the street and into a four-strand barbed wire fence. He suffered multiple cuts from the wire.

The new bike was totaled with a bent fork, destroyed light; front fender ripped loose and numerable deep scratches. I don't remember what ever became of that beat-up new/old bike, but I do remember the hurt when I came home that day.

Quit My First Job

First job I quit happened when I was about 12 (1940). I was offered the job from an old fisherman on the Missouri river in his wooden john-boat, handling trammel nets as they were being raised into the boat with fish in them. I was enthralled with the possibility of riding in the boat up and down the river and would have traded most anything for the adventure, and besides he said he could pay me if the catch was good. As I recollect this, not a second thought was given to my safety such as a life preserver. The Missouri river is muddy and very swift in some places plus the old john boats floor inside was slick with wet mud and dripping water from nets. It was necessary to stand up when rolling a net into the boat far enough to retrieve the fish from it. I weighed probably just over 100 lbs. at that time, and had been swimming many times in the back waters with other boys in the neighborhood. I had developed little fear of the treachery the river could offer.

Our first net retrieval was only about a 5-minute boat ride upstream from home port at which time we tied up to the anchored trammel net line. "What a disappointment!" "Only a few minutes ride!" But then the old guy began yelling orders as the net was being raised, *"grab that hoop and lean back"*, *"c-mon, don't let that fish flop back in the water"* and etc. It didn't take me long to realize that maybe fishing wasn't for me after all, but I thought we would likely return to port since we had caught some fish. Instead we moved up stream about five more minute's ride and repeated the net raising thing again and again. Many time's we would raise a trammel net finding nothing in it so he decided to return to home port (which was nothing more than two trees, some bench boards and a smoothed-out mud bank at the river). There was a customer waiting for fish which chilled my anticipations. We hadn't gone more than 500 yards from home port and by this time I was very disappointed in the lack of boat riding especially since the boat net was towing a "catch net" overboard so as not to drown the fish and we were sort of floating back downstream.

I offered to help transfer fish from the boat drag net, but he said "*You watch, cause I don't want you to lose any of them*" while he put most of the fish except for two in a live box at the water's edge at home port.

"*OK, kid I'll show you how to dress fish so, you carry one and I'll take the other*". These were carp fish about 20" long and they still flopped around, so he quickly showed me how to put my fingers in the gills to carry it. I'm pretty certain I don't like this job by now but my mom had always said **"If a task is once begun never stop until it's done".**

We departed to his river bank outdoor business office carpeted in dry mud, fish scales and sand décor. Huge willow trees provided columns for holding some driftwood boards nailed across forming a cleaning bench. Both fish suffered fatal blows to the head, then scraped vigorously sending flying scales all around, and opened up to disgorge their inside components. Flies attacked the cleaning board and fish insides. The old fisherman sent me to the river with two buckets for cleaning water and my bare feet could hardly support the extra weight on the way back in the mud. The fish bodies had been quickly wrapped in the local Banner News-paper and given to the waiting customer.

"*All right kid, we will go across the river now to run the other nets*". However, as I had anticipated riding the boat all over the river, a life-saving circumstance cheated me, or saved me from becoming a professional fisherman. The old fisherman's wife showed up and he decided to take her instead of me. I rode my bike home and failed to report for work the next day.

Foolish Boys on The River

St. Charles MO is located on the Missouri River a few miles from its conflux with the Mississippi River. The river runs due north at that point and is generally about a half-mile wide during normal water flow. However, when flooding times come the river will spread to considerable widths and sometimes flood riverside homes. My parents were renting a small house located atop a small bluff, about 1-½ miles south of town on the river road. Between our house and the river was the M. K.T. (Missouri, Kansas & Texas) railroad known as the Katy line.

In the spring of 1940 the river flooded all lowlands around us and was within a few inches of the top of the rails of the Katy tracks. Backwater was over the river road on our side of the tracks and afforded about a two-foot deep pool for my younger brother and I to play around in. We had located an old homemade mortar box consisting of a sheet metal bottom nailed to the edges of a pair of 2 X 8 boards. The old mortar that had remained in the box bottom sort of sealed what my brother and I considered a perfect boat about 8' long. We had cut a pair of young sapling elms and had nailed flat shingles to one end to make paddles and used the other end as a pole for shallow water navigation. We were busy with our "Lewis & Clark" discovering when an old guy walking on the Katy tracks approached us with a money-making proposition.

He said he lived in a stilted shanty just south of us on the riverside of the Katee tracks about a ¼ mile from our house. The water had risen to a level just below his windows and was rushing forcefully around and under his home. He told us that if he helped us drag our boat over the tracks and launch it on the riverside we could float down (north) to the side of his house. Just inside the window was a suitcase on the kitchen table that he needed and he would give us fifty cents a-piece if we would recover it for him.

The water on that side was swift and deep so we couldn't use our pole and anyway the old mortar box boat needed to be bailed constantly to stay afloat. But we decided that the money was going to be easy and proceeded with the rescue plan. We made it to the house, and it was scary since the velocity of the water moved us very fast. When we arrived against the side of the house the current nearly overturned us under the building. We clung to the windowsill while the old guy shouted orders from the railroad tracks to abandon ship and get in the house.

While this was good advice we didn't want to lose our mortar box boat and face the consequences of explaining that to its owner. So, we grabbed the suitcase, baled water and launched off downstream working our way back toward the Katee tracks. Our return to civilization was pretty quick but had washed us considerably downstream before the old guy could assist us with dragging the boat back on our side of the tracks. He gave each of us a fifty-cent coin and advised us not to tell any-one about the incident.

We returned back home against the current by wading the backwater and pushing our boat before us, but Mom had been looking for us and we had to confess everything. She said that she was going to have Dad find the old guy and educate him right after he educated us. It turned out that the actual owner of the house was not the same person we had helped get the suitcase and we always wondered what the real story was.

Green Apples

In the summer of 1940 while living on the South River road I made friends with another boy my age and we kept pretty busy launching green apples from the end of a stick that had been sharpened to a point. If we stuck the apple just the right amount onto the stick, providing it was just the right size we could launch the apple with a certain degree of accuracy, (almost).

We had decided to use an old abandoned car for a practice target and were pretty busy hitting or missing the driver's window, which was imagined to be the spot where the bank robber would be sitting. The apple tree was beginning to lose most of the reachable ammunition, so we decided to climb up and harvest enough ammunition for the next attack. My mom saw us climbing up in the tree and proceeded to interrupt the action with a verbal outburst that scared my buddy out of his wits. He departed quickly for his trailer house home and I was left to face the music alone.

After some minutes of corrective verbiage (seemed like an hour) mom started back into the house which was several yards away.

I looked longingly at the pile of perfectly good ammunition that was going to waste away since I was instructed to come into the house immediately and she would find some constructive things for me to do. I decided to launch just one more apple, before reporting for whatever household duty was in store for me. I carefully stabbed the apple onto the stick intending to launch it for a distance shot. The wind up was perfect and the swing was "right on", however the apple failed to release until the swing was almost at its end. The apple sailed almost the speed of a professional base-ball pitchers throw and hit my Mom in the back at just about the belt line. After all these years, I can still see in my mind's eye this incident and remember my Mom falling face down on the gravel driveway.

I remember the trauma as I rushed to help her up and the tears we both shed. I remember how she forgave me for what she had first thought was retaliation for her interrupting our green apple on a stick game. I spent the rest of the day near her and could only imagine the punishment when Dad got home. However, Mom didn't tell on me and the guilt I suffered was probably worse than what my Dad's wrath would have been.

First Job Benefits

Fall of 1941 was my first-for-pay job at the Ritz movie theatre. Some of the guys I met down on the Missouri river banks told me that the theatre owner was looking for ushers. I went home and told Mom that I wanted to go to work. She laughed and said that it was OK with her but that I would need to dress up if I wanted the job and that I would need dress-up clothes if they hired me. I told her that if I was working, I could afford to buy clothes.

I walked into town wearing the best pants I had and a dress shirt that was Dads, a little big but not too bad and besides I had my hair combed and soaked with "Brilliantine" hair dressing. My interview was frightening especially when he began to ask me if I had ever sneaked into the show. The reason I was nervous was that I had knowledge about who had done this from talk among the guys on the river bank several times. He believed me when I said *"No"* and asked me if I would work from 7:00pm to 10:00 or 11:00pm three nights a week and sometimes for special shows on Sunday afternoon if needed.

My primary job was ushering and I was issued a flashlight with which to direct people to seats and flash anyone who was talking during the show. This was a little troublesome if some of my river buddies happened to be in the show without their parents. My pay rate was $.35 cents an hour and I could eat all the popcorn that I wanted. The money was great, but the fringe benefit was unbelievable since I had never been treated to store bought popcorn in my life. After the first couple of weeks work my take-home wages were about $4.00 per week, and I was eating at least six bags of popcorn a night.

At about the end of the first month the assistant manager stopped me as I came to work and told me that Mr. Lessing (owner) wanted me in his office sometime after the first show started and before the first reel change. I was so nervous that I could hardly point the flashlight for the people I was ushering, but I reported to the office as directed. Mr. Lessing seated behind his big desk proceeded to tell me that I was doing a good job, but he needed to make a change in order to hold down costs.

The cost containment change was as follows, *"You can still have all the popcorn you want, but you can have only __one bag a week to put it in__".*

Fired Upon

Living on the south river road nearly two miles out of town, the spring of 1940 brought flood waters to the Missouri river. A lowland area along the side of the river was covered with a few feet of back water and a houseboat family floated in next to the Katy railroad track. They tied the houseboat to some willow trees and after the flood waters receded the houseboat became a permanent residence, sort of like squatters. The south river road ran parallel to the railroad on the open land side. I attended school in town by walking first the river road then the streets in town to school.

The houseboat people were referred to as "river rats" and didn't seem to fit in to the neighborhood, but were tolerated never the less. They had a boy who was about my age who didn't attend school very often and I avoided him as much as possible.

One afternoon in the late fall of 1940, I was walking home after school accompanied by a girl my same age. The houseboat boy usually walked down the Katie tracks all the way from town, but for some reason he chose to walk the river road this day. He caught up with Mary and me roughly half mile out of town and attempted conversation with us using taunting insinuations. We ignored this as much as possible, and I told him to "*walk on the railroad and leave us alone*". We were within a short distance of his houseboat and he screamed "*you can't make me!*" but he had to leave the road anyway in order to get home. Our homes were farther down the road so we hurried away as he crossed the tracks and entered his houseboat screaming obscenities.

We had proceeded about another two or three hundred feet when he came out of his houseboat with a rifle. He shot some two or three times in our direction but his houseboat was lower than the railroad track and so was our road on the other side.
I can still remember the bullets singing through the surrounding willow saplings along the roadside. I glanced back to see his mother come out of the house and grab him by the hair and drag him back inside. I didn't see him after that, but rumor had it that he was sent to some kind of a reform school. We moved into town shortly after that and I think the houseboat left on the next flood.

Destiny Foretold

Sometime in the summer of 41 having moved into town on South Main Street, my mother had become friendly with a neighbor lady in the south main street area. This lady was a self-proclaimed "see'er" into the future and had fascinated my mom with her ability to predict the future. My Dad wasn't impressed with her and I overheard several discussions over the friendship.

One-day Mom insisted on my accompanying her to visit this lady. Her home was a little on the messy side. She was tall and dark completed, black hair pulled back and the most piercing brown eyes you can imagine. She greeted Mom as she prepared a cup of tea for them, but she scared me when she grasped my shoulder with considerable authority and stated matter of factual *"This young man is destined to become famous and I want to read his palm for you"*.

Mom agreed that she was also sure that I was destined for fame, but would she be able to predict the nature of my greatness? I think some money passed hands but it was done outside of my direct view. The lady then held my right palm up and began to trace lines and all the time she was mumbling about life lines, and pathways and she was especially interested in the calluses. (I rode a bike without grips many hours a day).

She finally stated that I would be a famous inventor or discoverer of new places or things. After having heard my destiny spelled out so positively, my ego went out of control for the next year or two. I haven't thought about this for many years but I guess you must have patience for the fulfillment of such predictions.

First Run-in with the Law

I had made friends in our new neighborhood that required some gathering time and B-B gun shooting meetings. I had a daisy air rifle that I was supposed to share with my brother. I had been up on Second street shooting at tin cans and was on my way home. Dad had always hammered into my head *"Never carry a loaded gun"* since he had lost his father to a gun accident when he was very young.

This time as I approached an intersection and realized that my rifle had been cocked, but wasn't sure if there was a B-B in the chamber. I decided to just swing the barrel up in the air and pull the trigger to clear the chamber. Unfortunately, there was still a B-B in the chamber and when fired (without aiming) I hit a street light bulb.

I was shocked as the glass showered down and my first inclination was to run home as fast as I could. An old guy with no shirt on was mowing his lawn and as I started to run he yelled at me *"Hey kid, stop in the name of the law"*. Not knowing quite what to do, I stopped and he made me sit down on the curb while he went into his house to retrieve his police badge. When he showed me this, I nearly fainted while he quizzed me as to where I lived. Since I only lived in the next block in a little house behind others, he proceeded to confiscate my rifle and escort me home.

Unknown to me he was the only policeman in the whole town (Squirrel Shafer) and he lectured my mom and me till it sounded like I might have to go to prison depending on whether or not the cost of damages was sufficient to warrant that. Mom was able to talk him out of the Daisy air rifle which I wasn't allowed to use for the next twenty years I think and when the costs of the city property were learned, I was to pay-up. We were never billed for anything and I still believe that Policeman Squirrel Shafer recognized my "anticipated" prison term as punishment enough.

South Main Explosive Experts

South Main Street was definitely a blue-collar neighborhood, however the economy had improved to the point that Mom and Dad both could get jobs. Mom worked several places and as I recall she worked in a dress factory and also in the shoe factory since the tomato factory was only good in the summertime. Dad drove trucks and worked as a punch press operator until he got a war time job making ammunition in what was known as the small arms factory in St. Louis.

He came home one time with a few 30 caliber detonator caps which were small brass containers about the size of a pea containing an impact explosive. Fascinated with the exploding noise it made if you hit one with a hammer I found out the hard way that small pieces of the brass would fly out when you did this. I was showing this off to couple of my buddies when a little brass shard became imbedded in Glen Bains ankle. He bled a little and as far as I know he wore that brass throughout his lifetime since we didn't dare divulge this to anyone.

As young boy's we occasionally found small explosive signals used by the railroad to signal locomotives as they ran over them. I remembered as a kid having experience with one of these. (see Boys Big Bang story) These devices consisted of a half dollar size cake of dynamite with two lead strips for fastening to a rail. Sometimes the lead strips would fail to hold the dynamite in place as the locomotive approached and would fall off the rail. When we were lucky enough to find one lying loose, we would fasten it to the rail just before the work crew came

in after working all day. It was fun to see the guys jump
when the "herdie girdy" ran over the explosive signal. We
only did this a couple of times since we heard that a railroad
detective was looking for thieves who had stolen signals
from the railroad

Bathing

Our house wasn't right on Main street it was back
behind the owner's house which sat out on the street. Our
house was an all brick building about 30' x 30' and had been
originally used in the old days as a blacksmith shop. It was
two rooms with an attic bedroom upstairs. There was no
water in the house, so we carried from an outside faucet on
the owner's house.

In the next block north of us was Packet's Barber
shop where you could rent a hot water shower, soap bar and
towel for 25 cents. There were two shower stalls in the back
room and one time when I was about 15 years old, a
circumstance of embarrassment took place as follows. I
wanted to shower and Mr. Packet told me to go ahead but
that another guy was in one of the showers. Sure-enough
when I went back there a grown man was showering while
his cloths were draped over a chair.

I had just gotten in the shower when a ruckus started
with a lady and Mr. Packet. It turned out that she was the
wife of the guy in the other shower stall who worked on the
railroad gang. His wife knowing that he was likely in the
shower, had decided to remove his paycheck money to
prevent him from spending it at the tavern down the street.
As far as I could tell she made good by taking his pants and
money over Mr. Packets objection. I didn't come out of the
shower until everybody left, but I heard that the guy had to
borrow a towel and left to go home in his shoes and a towel.

Cigar Smoker

Some-time in the summer of 1942 my Mom and we (kids) made a visit from St. Charles back to her home-town of Whitehall Ill. I think we went with my Dad in a borrowed car since we didn't have one. I hadn't seen my cousins for a long time and they were all growing up quite a bit. My cousin Junior who was three months older than me was now driving his big brothers truck on the sly since it had no key for the ignition. There were several other things that had taken place in the growing up process that gave me a slight amount of inferiority pangs.

After all, I was 14 now and childish things were no longer of as much interest. Anyway, Junior and I had walked to the other end of town to visit with our other cousin Gene who was three months younger than me. Across the street from Gene's house was the Cox family and the twin girls who was our age had certainly taken on new forms. I was interested in renewing acquaintance with our former playmates, but was told "forget it" since they were being monitored full time by their "old man".

However, it was Saturday the Cox family usually went downtown in the evening and sometimes the girls could be seen away from the guard. Junior and I decided to go to town after supper and hang out at the pool hall and watch for the Cox twins on the street. We spent about 3 fruitless hours (no sight of the girls) and finally the pool hall guy "kicked us out" or buy something.

Junior decided that we should just start back home since it was getting dark. He also decided to buy a nickel cigar for the trip home since he really enjoyed smoking now. He asked if I wanted one and I said *"sure"* even though I had never smoked anything. But you can't let girls and cousins grow up and leave you behind can you? So he bought two.

We started home and lit the cigars immediately, but there must have been something wrong with my cigar since it soon made me a little dizzy. Junior said maybe I was inhaling too much at one time so just puff little puffs and inhale only part of them. I needed to establish myself as grown-up so didn't let on that any-thing much was wrong. Somehow I needed to get this cigar over with so I decided to bite off part of it and claim my enjoyment for chewing tobacco, which I was sure that he had never done. He followed my lead and by the time we arrived home the backyard toilet received two very sick inhabitants. That was the end of my smoking career for the next two decades but I didn't give up looking for girls since I decided that most of them didn't like cigars either.

Money Making

After having survived the cigar escapade, I found myself financially embarrassed while visiting with cousins. A severe rain and wind storm had gone through town creating considerable downed trees all around. Cousin Junior suggested that we join all the clean up work that was taking place and he seemed to know who would pay us for picking up broken limbs and placing them on the side of the street. We landed some hand labor work that was paying each of us about forty cents an hour.

However, this lady also had some big Maple trees that had broken trunks and limbs that were to big for trash pick-up. These big pieces needed to be removed to the town dump site, so Junior quoted her a price of five dollars and we would remove these for her. I questioned him as to how he expected the two of us to drag these several blocks to the dump site. He informed me that he had no intention of dragging these by hand since his older brother owned a Dodge truck that was about twenty years old. He knew how to get it started without asking permission, so we commandeered the truck and some log chain.

We made about three trips to the dump and it looked like we were going to be wealthy, but the lady insisted on the last huge tree trunk be removed also. It was about as long as the truck and probably two foot in diameter with two or three broken limb stubs at the other end. Since we couldn't load it we decided to drag it behind the truck with the log chain hooked around the back axel. The lady agreed to another two dollars and off we started down the street. Every-thing was going pretty good as long as we were on the asphalt street, however the last block or so into the dump site was gravel and dirt. That's when the old Dodge began to snort and stall out about every ten feet. The end result was a family disaster because Junior had burned the cultch out and we had to abandon everything there. It was getting late in the afternoon and I was supposed to be at my other Aunt's house   Junior said he would collect our money and get his dad to borrow somebody's horse to pull the tree trunk the rest of the way and drag the truck home.

I have always been glad that I wasn't at Junior's house when he revealed his trucking activity. His brother and his Dad were furious about the situation and Aunt Fefa sided against us and awarded all our money to the truck owner brother. My Mom questioned me un- mercifully as to whether I had suggested borrowing the truck or not, and of course I didn't.

That's me on the left and Junior on the right. Gene in the middle didn't get in trouble since he wasn't involved this time only 3 Months difference in our age's.

Black Boy

My other cousin Gene couldn't understand why I was not entitled to my tree limb removal money, but he said if I wanted to earn some money I should talk to his dad who worked at the clay tile factory. I never could bond with my Uncle Goldie, mostly because he refused to call me by my real name or even just Bob. My dad's nickname was Jack and Uncle Goldie simply put Jack and son together and called me Jack'son. Anyway, he said he would get me a job unloading coal for firing the kilns. The coal came into the factory yard via railroad coal-car that had a trap door in the center. This door opened at a position over a chute that emptied into a three-sided pit where it was later removed for firing the kilns while baking the clay tiles.

A coal-car is probably sixty feet long and has walls about six feet tall as best I remember. Only the center part of the coal would dump into the chute which left both ends with a pile of coal to be shoveled by hand into the chute. I could get three dollars per car that I unloaded, so I agreed to give it a shot. My cousins sort of grinned when I told them about my next moneymaker. A couple days went by when Uncle Goldie said I should be ready to go to work with him next morning since they had two coal cars coming in that night. We were on the job next morning at six and I was issued a number nine grain scoop. I weighed about 125 lbs. at about 5'5" tall and had removed my good tee-shirt since I was told the job was a little dusty. The guy who took me to the job mentioned some-thing about being pretty skinny for the job which made me sort of irritated and determined to make six dollars pretty quick.

The first coal car had been placed over the chute and when the trap door opened up coal dust enveloped me like a cloud. I coughed a little and the guy handed me a handkerchief and said to be sure he got it back later. The coal poured out for a long time and when it stopped I was black from head to foot. I then grabbed my shovel and climbed over the side at one end. Stepping into the loose coal was kind of tricky since I needed to avoid falling thru the trap door, but the guy had told me to just stick my shovel into the coal using it like a brake. Meanwhile hang onto a rope that had been draped over the side which could be grabbed to keep from sliding into the open trap door. I made it to the door opening almost without incident but I was now completely covered with black coal dust powder. The first shoveling went pretty easy just around the door opening but as I progressed farther and farther away the sweat began to flow. By the time I had finished the first end I realized that six dollars was not going to be easily made.

I finished the first car in about four hours and climbed out of the car to look for the guy to have the next coal car brought to the chute position. He accommodated me by handing me a long steel pinch bar and he and I were obliged to shove these bars under the wheels and pry the car wheels into a forward motion. It surprised me that we could get the car moving faster and faster by pinching and pinching away on the wheels. First we moved the un-loaded coal car out of the way, however with considerably more effort on our part the loaded car had to be moved into emptying position over the chute.

This took us about an hour and he wanted to know if I wanted to stop work before unloading the 2nd car. I had decided that was foolish since the sun was really baking down by now. I was now educated about moving a railroad car with pinch bar.

I unloaded the second car in the hottest part of the sunshine day and if it had not been for the cake of coal dust all over my back, I think I would have been sun burned. Uncle Goldie brought my six dollars' home with him that night and wanted to know if I wanted to come back when the next coal came in. I thanked him and told him that I was going back to St. Charles in the next day or two, but I did over-hear him tell my Mom *"that Jackson boy is a good worker"*. A swim and a cake of soap in the little reservoir removed most of the black coal-dust except for my clothes for which Mom did the best she could.

Halloween Prank

When I was in my second year of high school, I made friends with a kid that was a year older than me named Bud. He was trouble just waiting to happen, but he was lots of fun and we managed to stay out of serious trouble in spite of ourselves. One Halloween night we decided that it would be funny if we "borrowed" a junk tire from the pile behind Joe Lyons filling station on 2nd street. St. Charles Mo. is on the bank of the Missouri river and the town's main street is nearest the river with 2nd street uphill, 3rd street farther uphill and so forth.

The river auto bridge terminated onto 2nd street, so we selected an old tire and rolled it up the hill from 2nd street to 3rd street. Our plan was to launch and free roll the tire back down the hill onto the river bridge just to see how far it would go on the bridge entrance ramp. We thought about what a car exiting the bridge would do if it were suddenly faced with a tire coming up the road, so we waited at the top of the hill until no cars were on the bridge. We very carefully aimed the old tire at the bridge entrance and sent it down the hill with a boosting take off.

The tire rolled faster and faster down the hill and pretty much stayed in the middle of the street until it reached the 2nd street intersection. It suddenly swerved from its intended bridge entrance, veered north, hit the curb then became air-born and crashed into a plate glass store front window of an empty building. We were mortified at what had happened and made fast tracks out of there heading for 4th, 5th, and as many streets as we could cover.

I worked at Joe Lyons filling station and the next day I learned that "some kids" had cracked a window across the street, but it had already been broken and taped so this just sort of speeded up the overdue repair job. Some of the old men while waiting for their cars, tried, convicted and hung those kids as I witnessed nervously.

Crime Doesn't Pay

The summer of 1943 while WW II was in full swing I was 14 years old. I and another boy (Bud Garrett) a free spirit kind of guy were always poking around town. All parents and adults were working feverishly in the War effort where they could. If you were lucky enough to own a car, it was of limited use because all gasoline was rationed. Most cars had an "A" sticker on the windshield allowed you to buy 4 gallons of gas per week from your book of "A" gas stamps. Almost every thing else was rationed such as meat, sugar and shoes.

Bud and I were pretty much on our own to wander at will around town on our bicycles. We had our favorite tours, for instance we sometimes decided to travel to the West End of town. The Missouri River borders the East Side and pedaling uphill was work. We could usually park on the side walk at 2nd street and wait for a trailer truck to turn the corner at Clay street for its gear grinding climb ascent uphill to the west. Each of us would grab onto a hinge on each side of the trailer and get a free tow uphill to about 5th Street. Many times an irate truck driver would stop and threaten us for hooking a ride, but we would just coast back down and wait for a more accommodating trucker.

We learned to drop off at about 5th street since the truckers would start to pick up speed and anyway this was very near the St. Charles Dairy plant. We learned to go into the alley behind the dairy and check the loading chute for a lodged quart of ice cream that failed to reach the truck during loading. If the ice cream was still frozen, we needed to consume it in large bites since we only had pocketknives to dig it out and it would almost always give us a toothache and headache. Perhaps fitting punishment for young criminals, but we always seemed to recover without long term effects.

Since this is only part of our criminal escapades, I need to divulge the following since it has had some lifetime effects. By checking behind businesses for anything of interest, you would be surprised at the treasures that can be found. A bridge crossed the Missouri river, which was the hi-way into St. Louis county and regular public bus service across terminated on the St. Charles side. The bus terminal building at 2nd street had a short order counter in which mostly breakfast was served for travelers waiting for a bus.

One day, Bud and I were poking around behind the bus terminal and discovered the back door was wide open into the back-basement room. Naturally, curiosity overtook our judgment so we peeped into the refrigerator just inside the door. Low and behold there in plain sight was several trays of pork sausage. Now remember, meat was rationed and it was seldom that you could get enough meat to meet your desires.

We decided to "borrow" one of the trays and present it to our Mom's, so we quickly departed with a whole tray of pork sausage in one of our bicycle baskets. Before we made it home we reassessed and decided that we better not divulge our accomplishment especially since we had no way of obtaining rationing meat points. So the only reasonable thing to do was to eat it ourselves.

Bud procured a skillet and I "borrowed "some bread and we proceeded to a place on the creek south of town. We built a campfire using his cigarette lighter and some dead wood and proceeded to consume the entire tray of pork sausage. I don't need to relate the next few days of bodily reactions, but to this day, I am unable to consume greasy sausage. Perhaps this is a fitting and lasting punishment for a former criminal.

Ritz Rabble-Rousers

The following stories take place at one of the three movie houses in St. Charles Mo. when I was a teen age boy. The Strand theatre was the biggest in town and considered the "hi hat" place to be. The Strand had more seating capacity than both the other movie houses (Roxy and Ritz) including its balcony. The Ritz theatre located on the east side of South Main street, in the blue-collar area of town, was the gathering place for many of the guys and girls our age. The Ritz provided part time jobs for four or five of us boys, my first real job being usher and clean-up. The Ritz had the typical sloped floor, two aisles with six seats each side, twelve in the middle and fourteen rows. I can remember vividly the seating because I swept the floor many times starting in the back and progressing down to the front (screen area) pushing popcorn, bags, candy wrappers and sometimes a wad of bubble gum (providing I hadn't stepped on it first).   Occasionally we floor sweepers would come upon a coin or two and even a wallet, (always empty) since it likely was lost by some kid who having spent his bankroll was careless about putting it back in his pocket.

Found Wallet

This brings me to a first story of several. Mr. and Mrs. Lessing, the owners maintained a 'lost and found' box in the office where we were required to place all found items until the owner would reclaim the item. The Ritz building was flanked on the South by Mr. Sherdings grocery store and an empty lot on the North side except for two large bill board signs facing main-street. The bottom two feet or so of these bill board signs ware trimmed in lattice work providing a perfect place to hide behind and spy on pedestrians as they came and went along the sidewalk.

My buddy Pierce (nicknamed Goon Dog) and I conjured up a fun plan which constituted of an unclaimed wallet from the lost & found box and on which we attached a long string. A few minutes before the first show let out (about 9 pm) we would place the wallet on the sidewalk in front of the bill board signs carefully stretching the string along a crack and across the cinder lot and through the lattice work under the billboard sign.

We would then lay in the darkness on our bellies and wait for a victim. When the first show let out, some people would just simply pass by the wallet while others would see it but hesitate to pick it up, thinking that the owner was nearby. We sometimes would catch a mature lady bending over to retrieve a found treasure right in front of people scurrying to get home. This was always the most enjoyable catch and just as the lady's hand was about to grab the prize, we would jerk the string and snicker to ourselves. The lady would always be embarrassed especially if she had impeded the pedestrian traffic.

All this went well for a few laughs but the word soon got around and a pair of smart-butt neighborhood guys teamed up. When they came upon the wallet, one stepped on it while the other stormed around the far end of the billboards. We anticipated the counter attack and retreated very quickly farther into the empty cinder lot and hid under the loading dock for the grain building next to the Katy rail road until safe passage was established. We heard by the grapevine that the guys had anticipated a cash discovery in the wallet.

Stinky Revenge

Joe Broyles (nicknamed Gimpy) was a very gentle kid and one of the three big Baum brothers was continually picking on Joe. Most-times this was a big-time guy bullying an easy mark who had no dad to help with corrective action. It was middle of the winter and the Ritz had a stoker fed coal furnace in a room behind the screen. The room was just big enough for the stoker and furnace with room on one side for a couple of wheelbarrows. This room was completely lined with sheet metal which was actually a plenum chamber with an exhaust fan on top which blew warm air into the theatre each side of the screen. (NO IT WOULDN'T PASS CODES)

One day the big Baum (nicknamed, Wimpy) was in the theatre lobby up front while Joe and I were supposed to go to the stoker room and clean out all the red-hot clinkers into the wheelbarrows. There were doors into and out of the furnace room both with dead bolt locks. The street-side door for the front lobby was key-locked and Joe had the key. He was up-set because Wimpy had beat on him earlier, so we devised a retaliatory plan.

After we loaded the stoker hopper with coal we then removed all the red hot furnace clinkers into a wheelbarrow. Instead of taking the wheel barrow out the backdoor we turned on the blower, and **urinated** into the wheelbarrow of red hot clinkers and retreated to the outside leaving Wimpy locked in the building <u>with no key.</u>

Cry Room

The above stinky incident reminds me of another situation that occurred occasionally at the Ritz when we

119

were to be cleaning the show. Located at the back of the show just inside the audience seating area was a small room off to one side that had a large glass window facing the movie screen and a door that could be closed. This room provided about four chairs and enough floor space to accommodate baby baskets for ladies whose babies were crying during show time.

Some times this room was also used as a privacy space for an occasional guy who was lucky enough to talk his movie date inside, providing Mr. Lessing wasn't there and the room was not being used by some fussy baby. This situation was mostly in the imagination of the guys and was the topic of several conversations at clean-up time.

However, the most unimaginative situation occurred when one of us would discover that the room had been used the night before by a baby wearing a torn rubber panty and left the damaged dirty diaper overnight. Usually there was a full fledged labor strike over who had the cry room to clean up.

Ritz Opportunity

14 years old and working at the Ritz theatre in St. Charles made me a fairly rich man since I was making over $12.00 a week. The Ritz made almost endless possibilities for meeting girls that were not in our public-school system. The Catholic Church had a rather large high school and the word was out that the girls who went there were boy starved since the Nuns were pretty strict. WW II was in full force and theaters were a favorite means of catching up on the war news. Since I was an usher one of the favorite methods of approach was when a girl or two came, (usually with a mother) we would try to seat the girl next to the aisle. My best friend Pierce (Goon dog) and I had spent considerable

time planning this and sometimes it worked (but most time it only gave us failure to talk about the next day).

Our work station was near the rear seating row, since we were issued a flashlight and our job was to find seating for anyone who came in after house lights were out. One of our fringe benefits was all the popcorn we wanted, so we would always have a full bag of popcorn stashed just behind the last seat, to be used as girl bait, in case one showed up. Generally, the girl or girls depending on the situation would visit the concession stand at some point during the evening and we devised a sure fire approach plan. The plan was to start conversation usually like this as they came into the concession area.

"Could I ask you something?" most times we would get a cold stare, **BUT** occasionally

"What"

"I bought this bag of popcorn, but I am not supposed to eat it while working, would you
mind holding it for me until I get off.

The Gold-Digger

"I wouldn't mind holding the popcorn for a little while, but I might eat some of it, if it's OK with you."
"Sure it's OK, and I don't think I will need to usher much longer, so I'll just pick up the bag pretty soon."

I watched as she returned to her mothers' seat and I could tell she asked permission to sit farther back in the seating. She took the second seat in from the aisle *holy cow!*

It wasn't long before I managed to get one of the other guys to watch my aisle. I went to the row behind and occupied a seat directly behind her. I could tell she knew I was behind her, but I leaned close to her and whispered.
"I'm Bob and you are holding my popcorn".

121

She turned her head and whispered back

"I'm sorry, but I ate a lot of it"

"It's OK, I'll go get some more" and before she knew it, I was back with two bags.

Upon my arrival, I asked if I could sit in the seat next to her and presented her with her own popcorn. A few minutes later, (whispering) I asked her name and she said *"Arlene"*

At this time the two ladies in front of her turned and loudly SSSSHED us. Being an executive of the establishment my reputation for keeping order was in jeopardy, so I wasn't able to make much more progress with my ambitions that evening. However, after the show was over, I managed to tell her that, I worked every Monday, Wednesday and Friday.

Sure enough she began to come to the show a couple times a week, but always with an older sister or her girlfriend. They were only to glad to allow her to sit in the last row next to where my job required me to stand. I always made sure she had popcorn and after a couple of weeks, I asked her if she would like go to the Strand Theater with me on Saturday afternoon. I spent over $3.00 that day. I don't know how she was able to ditch her big sister but I became infatuated with her.

So much so, that I would run as fast as I could from my public school to within two blocks of the Catholic school and wait for her to come by so I could walk her home. It didn't matter that this was at least ½ mile out of the way for me. My infatuation grew and grew, remembering now that it hurt my heart just to think about her. Christmas time was about a month away and I decided that I was going to buy her a gold locket for Christmas.

My keeper wages were about $7.00 weekly since I paid $5.00 at home and I was buying my own clothes, so the locket price of $18.00 was considerable. Christmas came and I gave her the locket and she gave me a kiss in the cry room and a promise that my picture would be inside the locket after she got one from me. It was at least a couple of weeks before I saw her again and she acted kind of strange, sort of like she didn't know me. She came to the Ritz on a week night and I asked if I could walk her home. She said OK but she had something to tell me. I felt a certain un-comfortableness and sure enough when we got to the back door of her home she told me that she had a boyfriend from another school and he was jealous.

Her Dad came to the door before I could protest and demanded that she come in immediately. I found out later that her family had interceded into her friendship choices for a couple of reasons, religious and money that my Dad owed her Dad's grocery store. After the hurt went away I always felt she could have given the hard earned locket back, but that's the way it is sometimes. Later my buddy "Goon-dog" asked me about her once and I threatened to punch him out if he didn't shut up.

This is a new girl (Betty) I introduced to the Ritz gang, Mr. Lessing in ticket booth & Goon-dog my buddy. (see "Captured" story)

123

At this point the situation could progress or digress, however this writing is about ---

Chapter Nine:

No More Kid Stuff

Captured

In the summer (1944) before my senior year of high school, I had been working at Joe Lyons service station and Rauch Lumber in St. Charles MO. I was making my own money and was planning to buy a car so I could travel on my own. Meantime, once in a while a buddy "Bill" and I would board a passenger bus to St. Louis and stop at Westlake Amusement park across the river. The park had a skating rink, a fun house, several kiddy rides and a roller coaster ride.

My buddy Bill and I were cruising the midway one afternoon, looking for girls when we spotted a couple we had seen before at St. Charles high school. My buddy said *"hey that one is a sweetie, lets pick-em up and go for a ride on the roller coaster"*. His approach was receptive by one girl, but the other one was not too interested in riding the roller coaster with me. However, she finally decided that waiting around while the rest of us had fun riding was not acceptable.

So, we boy's bought tickets and the four of us boarded the ride. Bill and his pick-up girl were seated in front while the pick-up girl beside me settled in the back together. This was perfect, because I envisioned stealing a kiss and anticipated her delightful reception of my ambitions, while no one would be able to see.

As the ride cars began to climb the first steep incline, Bill's girl was probably frightened so he put his arm around her. I immediately followed suit and was promptly shoved away and notified that she was not afraid, *"so keep your hands on your side!"* Disappointed at the rejection, we barely spoke on the ride. We managed to exchange names and rode the bus together back to town where I "dumped her" to get home on her own even if she was pretty.

What are you interested in?

I wonder what they are interested in!

This could be interesting!

I think she has made a choice...

others were still looking

Fishing is interesting
This is what always interested us!

128

It was only a few days later while working at Joe Lyons filling station that I spotted the hard-to-get girl walking down the street to the bus station lunch counter at noon time. She whistled a tune as she walked along and wore a barrette in her beautiful wavy hair. I made it a point to be at the filling station several days at noon time even if it was my day off to watch her walk by for lunch. I found out that she worked at the Kroger store a block down the street

I stopped her one day to say *"Hi"*, and asked if she would like to go swimming at the city park pool with me sometime. She was healthy looking and I was sure that I would enjoy seeing her in a bathing suit. She accepted the invitation and told me where she lived. I lived on south main-street, she lived on the west side of town and the pool was located on the north side of town. So, I put several walking miles on this body just for a date on the chance that she would be more receptive. Chance became a reality and the miles were nothing compared to the miles and 60 plus years we have traveled since as "Bob & Betty".

Not sure who got <u>captured</u> but the roller coaster ride thru life is still underway.

She gave me this picture for my wallet later that summer???

Well-Dressed Crook

Working at Joe Lyons auto service station (new job after the Ritz) was hard and dirty work since my job consisted mostly of working in the pit greasing the under body fittings or draining oil pans. However, there were some joyful duties like driving customer cars around to the rear of the building and picking up another one for washing or greasing. Since I was not old enough to drive on the streets, I was tutored by Joe's brother-in-law to use only two gear positions low, reverse and the clutch. I was warned over and over never to touch the gas pedal, so my driving was confined to the property, and my feet were confined to the clutch and brake pedals. This was good training as it turned out since learning how to gently engage the clutch at idle speed on various cars prepared me for street driving later on.

Joe was a heavy drinker and much of the time he was drunk by noon since he was worried about being drafted into the war according to his brother-in law. The "new tire" rack hung from the ceiling with rubber radiator hoses hanging below it. Joe wore the coin changer on his belt with paper money in his pocket, and when he became inebriated he used the radiator hoses as handles to hold him up. When I needed to make change for a customer's gasoline buy, Joe was not always correct when dispensing coins. His brother-in-law had told me, *"just put the mistake money in the pedestal desk"* since Joe would become belligerent if his mistakes were pointed out.

One-day Joe and I were working the station when a man dressed in a suit and driving a late model Packard car came in and started conversation with Joe while I was busy repairing some tires left from the day before. Joe called me in from the shop and told me to fill the Packard with gas and park it out of the way while he and the man had a drink together. When I went inside and reported the gas cost, the man handed Joe a fifty- dollar bill. Joe couldn't make change, but I overheard the man tell him that he owned several trucks that would be in for gasoline. They were a roving carnival on their way across the river to Illinois and an agreement was made, after a few drinks, too have the truck caravan just drive through and fill up. The man left the $50.00 bill and drove back to wherever his carnival was preparing for the move. (You could buy 4 to 5 gal of gas for a dollar in those days!)

Joe was elated at the prospect of the business, so the next hour or so was dedicated to more celebration drinking. The suit dressed man showed up for another drink and I was given instructions to start a gas pump and not turn it off between trucks. The last truck would have the money to pay everything over the fifty dollars. The next hour was consumed with trucks loaded with all kinds of carnival paraphernalia wandering in being several minutes between sometimes. I not only filled trucks, but also an occasional stationary power engine for a carnival ride. The suit man had left to go check on the last truck after a few minutes

After a while I began asking drivers where the last truck was and I was told it's on the way. Joe was pretty drunk by this time and I was pretty sure that the last truck had been gassed up, but didn't have any way of knowing for sure. I finally turned off the pump and tried to reason with Joe that the man with the money was probably not coming back. Joe finally agreed to let me call his brother-in-law. I am not sure if Joe ever got the money, but the most devastating circumstance was that since gasoline was rationed due to WW2, replacement gasoline could not be obtained without ration.

Indecent Exposure

We were all in our teens, over running with energy and love of social experiences that celebrated the release of parental oversight while lacking recognition of adulthood soon to envelope our existence. The Missouri river had flooded a few years before, after having been some-what confined by efforts of Governmental wisdom to restrict its natural course. The river had overflowed and created a whole new path across what was normally a County road plus open farmland. After flood disaster had subsided and the sizeable washout had settled into a very nice lake area became known as Grau's cut. This having a small beach was eventually supplied with some small buildings for swimmers to change into or out of swim-ware.

Our little group of (Ritz Gang) decided to load up a couple or so cars with the necessities for a swim and beach party at Grau's cut. This was a guys and girl event consisting of some who were dating and some "wanna-bes". My best lifelong friend Clarice was dating her boyfriend Clarence who eventually became her husband. Now Clarence was a very intelligent young man and was by nature more reserved and polite than most of the rest of us. Clarice on the other hand was a very well-endowed beauty and was impetuously inclined to do what was on her mind and adjust after, if judgment prompted her to do so. Some had worn street clothes bringing bathing attire along to change into should the party evolve into a swim rather than just beach bumming. This story is intended to point up another evolvement of the social acceptance of proper apparel in public.

Soon after everyone had arrived, some of the "wanna-be" Guys urged every-body to go into the shallow water for a beach ball game. Most of the Guys were receptive and likely were anticipating a sightseeing session of one-piece bathing suits that were beginning to give away to two-piece adornment. Clarice was wearing street clothes and being among the receptive beach ball enthusiasts quickly ducked into a small building to change into her bathing suit. Clarence being self-appointed stood just outside the building as territorial guardian, I suppose.

A few minutes passed and suddenly the door swung open and out popped Clarice clothed in her skirt but without her blouse and only her brassiere covering the top half. She was seeking help from one of her girl-friends with a jammed zipper or something. A couple or three of us Guys gaped at the unexpected beauty-personified while Clarence's face turned vivid red with disapproval, began chiding her. Clarice retreated back into the building in embarrassment and seemed to remain there for a while probably trying to overcome the social embarrassment which today would hardly be noticed.

First Car

I had just turned 16 years old and had a job working in the Standard Oil filling station fixing flat tires. I overheard a conversation about a 1928 model "T" car sitting in an old barn about 30 miles west of the town. I gathered all the money I could get together and hitchhiked rides to see if I could buy the car. I arrived at the farm with great expectations about owning my own car. After talking to the old lady who owned the place, I was considerably under financed for the $75.00 she was asking. I believe she could read my disappointment and offered to hold the car until I could get the rest of the money (about $45.00 I think). She told me that the car had not been started for some time, but that it was equipped with a self-starter "Delco" kit. It would need a battery and gasoline and air in the tires (since it was sitting on wood blocks). I was beginning to have second thoughts about the entire arrangement but she seemed to be anxious to sell me the car if I would just leave the money as a good faith deposit.

I hitchhiked back home after leaving the money and began to worry about how to get money, battery and gasoline together. Good fortune seemed to come my way when the owner of the filling station where I worked let me in on a little-known secret for rejuvenating a car battery. He gave me a dead battery that had been traded in by someone. (All the battery acid is first emptied into a big glass-baking dish, then the battery is flushed with water until the plates are cleared of debris, replace the acid and if you are lucky the battery is ready for a second life.)   I was also able to obtain an unsecured loan for the rest of the car money and a neighbor of the farm lady car owner offered to drop me off next Saturday afternoon with battery, 2 gallons of gas and a buddy of mine who knew how to drive.

By the time we got there and finished getting the car roadworthy it was already turning dark outside. When we let the car down off the blocks, all the tires were mostly flat, but we hand pumped them up. After several attempts we got the engine started and began our return trip with one working headlight, two leaking tires (good for about 3 miles) and an abundance of determination. Many tire pumping stops were made and early spring time mosquitoes nearly ate us at each stop plus we were starving for food. There were no more than half dozen other cars on the road during that trip and several times we wondered, if in the small hours of the morning, where help would come from if the engine suddenly quit, but we made it.

Next morning my Dad's comment was *"well, son you bought yourself a lemon"* but I didn't care what he thought because, I could fix every-thing up that it needed. This brings me to the rest of the story---

Dead Battery and the "T"

In the few months of Model T ownership Betty and I would ride around town in the evening occasionally. One evening we drove outside town just before dark and parked in an overlook wide spot along the river. The view was enjoyable and we found ourselves discussing our future ambitions and expectations. We were both working at the shoe factory in town and we had many dislikes to discuss about the working conditions there.

Darkness came upon us and we decided we should return to town and home since tomorrow was a work day. Low and behold when I attempted to start the engine the battery went dead after a couple of attempts. Betty was concerned about the situation but I assured her that if we just sat there for a while the battery would regain some of its charge and I was sure the engine would start then. I was truly sincere in my belief that this was the way it would work out if we would just sit still for a while. She accepted my knowledge and we proceeded to wait another hour or so, but the engine failed to start again.

By this time desperation set in and I felt it was not reasonable to think about walking all the way back into town. I asked Betty to get in the driver's seat and steer the car into a position that would get it back out on the gravel road where I might get a push from someone. We finally accomplished this but nobody came along to help.

The only other solution I could think of was for Betty to stay in the driver seat and push down on the low gear pedal when and if I could push the car fast enough to cause the engine to turn over and start. The biggest problem with this was two fold, Betty had never driven this car and if it started she must be able to hold the foot pedal in its neutral position while the engine was running. The other problem, there was only a few feet of level road and then uphill and I only weighed about 125 lbs.

It took two tries and finally the engine roared into life, but Betty was in the driver's seat holding the foot pedal in neutral while I was hanging on the outside. I knew that she had to move over to the passenger side without allowing the foot pedal to engage drive position especially since I had set the throttle far beyond idle speed. If we killed the engine, all would be lost and we would be relegated to walking several miles.

I was pleased to discover that Betty was pretty sharp at understanding our situation and we managed to maneuver ourselves without killing the engine. I drove her home considerably after dark and drove away thinking that I probably lost a girlfriend. I saw her the next day and she didn't say anything about the incident until many months later. It seems that when she told her Mom and Dad that I had asked her to just sit in the car until the battery charged up she received an education in car operation and had to defend the story as to what battery was being charged up, mine or the car?

Trade-in

After several months of "T" ownership and very few running miles without repairs I spotted a 1936 Dodge four door on a used car lot. The car lot was owned by one of my Dad's tavern buddies who had the reputation as a shrewd dealer in just about every thing, horse trader in the old days and now a used car dealer.

My model "T" was not running forward at the time due to a tiny misjudgment on my part a week or so earlier. The "T" transmission consisted of three flat faced wheels inside (low speed, high speed & reverse) around which a steel band lined with a belt would tighten when the driver depressed an appropriate floor pedal. These bands were subject to excessive wear and needed replacement often. The job was not particularly difficult since there was an access plate just under the wood floorboards. I had installed new bands, but had accidentally dropped a hex nut into the open transmission case. I attempted to recover the nut, but after many unsuccessful tries, I reasoned that the nut would just lie at the bottom of the case and never be missed.

Oh well so much for young logic, because during the first trip out, the nut lodged into the gears and destroyed forward motion. Fortunately, I could still have reverse and that is the way I was able to get home, <u>by backing up</u>. I parked the car in the back yard and reasoned that I should sell it and buy another.

I mentioned the 36 Dodge to my dad and he warned me not to deal with his tavern buddy and in his own words *"He'll skin ya just like that ole woman did"*. The used car lot was just around the corner from where we lived and the tavern was just across the street. Dad and his buddy were socializing when my dad asked him how much he was asking for that 36 Dodge. Dad asked how much trade-in he would give for my "T" and the man shook his head saying that he heard that my "T" wouldn't run.

After a few more refreshments an agreement was made that a trade-in was acceptable only if the "T" was driven onto the lot. Dad left the tavern, while his friend was engaged with others, staggered home, <u>backed</u> my "T" onto the lot and returned to the tavern. He then proceeded to finalize the agreement for the Dodge and I became the proud owner of another "lemon" with the help of refreshments and Dad's desire to out-fox the "horse trader".

Workers Entertainment

I am pretty sure that my Dad and Mom pressured me to get a job in the Shoe Factory since the work was supposedly steady and you could make extra bonus dollars if you worked hard. I wasn't particularly interested in factory work especially since my destiny in life had been foretold otherwise, but I needed money in great quantities or at least $30.00 a week. Being seventeen years old, I landed the job as a shoe-laster. The men's style at that time for leather dress shoes was known as "platform" shoes which consisted of an extra padded layer about ¾" thick between the sole and the upper portion.

The job as a shoe laster consisted of pulling a leather cover over the platform filler material and attaching it in place. The job required using one hand with pliers and the other hand to hand staple the tight leather down. The shoes were brought to your work station on wheeled racks about four feet high and held about 2 dozen shoes. The extra bonus money over your hourly wage rate was tabulated by the work week end and if you exceeded your quota you made bonus.

The problem was, that bonus quotas were dependent on product demand and more often than not Fridays were many times "shoeless" paydays using the polite factory language. The place was a sweatshop and being young and full of hope I was not overjoyed with the job, but while I always met my quota I began to whistle tunes to break up the monotony of the day.

One morning I was busy lasting shoes like crazy and whistling away the boredom when an entourage of big-shot management came touring the workplace. They stopped right behind me for a look-see, but I just kept whistling and working, probably ignoring them. Apparently, this irritated the General Superintendent because he reached over the shoe rack, took hold of my shoulder and said so all the other big-shots could hear *"Hey kid, if you want to be in show business you need to go to Hollywood"*.

As they walked away chuckling, I began to steam. I decided right then to quit in the middle of a shoe rack. I proceeded to catch up to the group, took the Superintendent's hand and placed the laster pliers in it, saying *"you can finish my rack, I'm going into show business"*. My Mom was mortified when the tongue wagers at the factory spread the story, likely jealous of my courageous put-down of the big boss.

Motorcycle Cycle

Being an almost adult young guy sometimes creates "macho" thoughts, desires and foolish undertakings that can get dangerous and costly in variable cases. In my case the "macho" situation in me came about because a friend my age became a motorcycle owner and had implanted sheer thoughts of being footloose and enviable. My friend and the cycle salesman provided me with kind hearted indebtedness and a 1932 well used Harley Davison.

I had never driven a motorcycle before but I happened to have an older motorcyclist cousin who was more than happy to appraise my machine and show me a few things. I need to touch lightly on his personality of habitual drunkenness and desire for attention. He was among the few to wear a tattoo as well as being a braggart.

He mounted my Harley, cranked the engine to nearly top RPM. Then engaged the clutch causing the back wheel to lay a black tire track nearly a half block long. I stood in complete amazement and shock at what my machine could do if you knew how, but I excused him as politely as I could.

My friend came by shortly after the before mentioned show and gave me enough beginner clues about learning to ride sensibly. After a few days of slow and sensible riding mostly in the alley I decided it was time to try hi-way riding. I made it thru town with no problems and couldn't help but notice car drivers not wanting to follow me, so a time or two, I was passed by them by speeding up and going around me in a close place.   The hi-way north of town was straight as a string in crop bottom land level into the next little town about four miles away. Upon exiting the city limits I decided to see what this machine could do, so I carefully opened the throttle. An immense thrill of feeling air blowing my hair and lips flapping against my teeth and being urged to lean my body (125 lbs.) into the handle bars was thrilling beyond expectations. There was no windshield to deflect air or anything else for that matter and helmets were unheard of, so you could enjoy the sensation of speed like a bullet. I had cruised about two or three thrilling miles, opening the throttle more and more, when I dared to glance down between my legs at the speedometer. The needle was climbing past the 105 MPH mark and climbing almost casually toward the top 120 MPH pin. The realization of what I was doing shattered my sensational joy and a sudden heart pounding scare enveloped me. I throttled back and promised myself never to disclose this except in the company of braggarts.

My machine was aged and soon began to show some mechanical deficiencies such as having to crank down time after time with my right leg to create ignition spark. Believing in my mechanical prowess, I decided to install a new set of ignition points and unfortunately, I installed them exactly upside down. I then decided to take a little ride, jumped aboard and stiff legged kicked down to start the engine. The down kick pedal moved all the way down, then backfired, thrusting my stiff right leg back up catapulting my body head first right over the handle bars.

Within an hour my right ankle and lower leg was nearly the same size as my upper leg. Mom and half-dozen other ladies evoked a medical cure procedure consisting of a five-gallon bucket of warm water laden with Epsom salts.

After a few weeks and a mechanical friend both my motorcycle and I were repaired, so I decided to pick up Betty at her work place. The alleyway was between buildings, so I was waiting at the door sitting on my machine, motor running and reviving it from time to time (listening to that sound was nearly spiritual).

I had sat there for what seemed an hour and I knew she would pop out that door any minute. So, I pushed the "suicide clutch" down with my left foot and engaged the manual gear shift into low gear so I could be ready to go anytime. All this readiness was being supported with my right foot on the ground, but an unexpected change to the left caused me to remove my left foot from the clutch and the machine leaped into propulsion. It shot forward a few feet and the left sissy bar plowed into a parked car causing my cycle to flip over on the right side. The accelerator hand grip became instantly rotated fully and I was nearly pinned under the 800 lb. machine spinning around and around on it's right side sissy bar allowing the back tire some traction while touching the gravel driveway.

I literally crawled on my hands and knees in the cindered driveway as fast as I could since the motorcycle was spinning around and around spitting cinders and dust in all directions. It made about three full revolutions before running out of fuel. I regained my composure somewhat as a crowd began to gather. I was bleeding on both palms, both knees and mostly in confidence, however after talking to a very sympathetic car owner (he let off) as to damage, I rode the undamaged motorcycle a few blocks home.

There are a couple more incidents, however I won't bother to bore the reader further since I really need the company of cycle addicts to impress.

My motorcycle friend mentioned earlier lost his life in a horrible accident and I decided to remove that possibility by selling my motorcycle.

Chapter Ten:

Married and Family Happenings

Mittler Acres-- St. Charles MO.

First Home

Just think, no subdivision development regulations, no zoning requirements, no building permits no interference if you thought you could do-it OK- just do-it.

Betty and I decided not to have children until we had a home of our own. We were both Eighteen when we married and we also decided to have as much fun as we could afford. It was close to four years of married life before we came across a property owner who had literally scraped a dead-end road in a circle on about 80 acres just about 3 miles south of town. He divided this into small acreage building sites and was selling them on contract for home sites, so we bought one. Thanks to a loan from Aunt Hattie & Uncle Harry.

We were renting an apartment in town for $15. a week which was more than we could afford so we decided to start a home on our acreage property. Our home furnishings consisted of a refrigerator, a folding bed and a kerosene cook stove acquired for the rental of two upstairs unfurnished rooms in an old couple's home. Unfortunately, we were asked to leave because they didn't care for the disturbance of sharing their home. I had invited a (down on their luck) cousin and wife to stay with us. That's why we emotionally decided to pay the bigger (double) rent mentioned earlier.

I had previously worked during High School for the lumber yard in town so I approached the owner to sell me enough lumber to build a 12 X 20-foot garage. He remembered me and instructed his manager to sell me the lumber on credit with an agreement that we make payments every week.

We were the first to start a structure near the back of that subdivision where there was no electric service. Consequently, I had to hand cut all lumber by hand. I had no previous building experience, so I must admit to many unusual carpentry techniques. The shell structure finally was under roof so we moved in with unfinished walls, no electric, no water and no heat but no more rent payments. We were overjoyed and proud of our ownership of this heavily mortgaged home.

We invested in a couple of five-gallon milk cans and carried water from town for kitchen and drinking use. My new found carpentry skills were put to use making a one-hole toilet building over a hand dug hole in the ground behind our new home. Spit-baths were conducted in an oblong galvanized wash tub and usually I got second use of the water.

Incidentally our payments to the lumber yard were never missed but oft-times we needed to limit our grocery buying. One time I recall our entire month's diet consisted of boiled great northern beans and bread, but this really didn't bother me to much since I had some childhood practice. Betty canned food from our hand dug vegetable garden on the two-burner kerosene stove and stored some of it in the new Norge (no electric yet) refrigerator bought while in the old folks town apartment.

Hauling water nearly every day in milk-cans hastened a decision to hand dig a cistern and waterproof plaster the clay wall for holding water. Every evening and a few weekends were consumed in excavation and dirt removal. A plywood cover was made with a small access door for dropping a roped bucket in for water removal. Eventually we invested in a cistern pump, hand operated of course. It was so very nice just to step out the back door and pump a bucket of kitchen water, but there was always the cost of having to buy a truck load of water.

Considerable time living in Mittler acres went by before we finally got electricity. We eventually finished the inside walls before our first child was born requiring us to change our original plan of the building as a future garage. We decided to add more room and then again as time went by yet another room over a hand-dug basement adjacent the house which entailed both the digging and laborious task of dirt removal. Another unforgettable lesson was learned as follows.

Since the clay basement walls were very nicely hand-dug shapes I decided this clay wall could serve as the outside form wall for concrete necessitating only to build forms for the inside of the walls. Recognizing a need to provide bracing to hold the forms vertical, I "X" braced the forms from the top of the walls down to the bottom of the opposite wall since the basement was small enough to span across. Again, working by ourselves we called for concrete and the driver simply uttered "oh-oh" as the first concrete poured into the form bottom and pushed its opposite form top in, resulting in finished walls to be about 2 ft. thick at the bottom and about 2 in. thick at the top. However, this basement provided space for a genuine oil fired furnace and I learned the hard way to be a heating expert of which I better not comment.

Cocker Spaniel dogs were popular as pets at that time and I was offered a full grown Cocker from a person that I worked with. We took the dog that happened to be pregnant with the thought that we could sell the pups and make money. Sure enough "Bell" the dog had eight pups and we were overjoyed at the prospects of big money, however we soon came to realize the pups needed to have their tails docked. We inquired as to the veterinary costs and were amazed at what this would amount too. True to form the old belief of, if you can't afford something just do it yourself, kicked in, and I docked them all myself.

This same philosophy applied to three small pigs I had acquired with the thought of growing them to butchering size for the meat and selling off the extra for money to pay for fence, and feed costs. We were overwhelmed at the possible veterinary cost for castration of one of the shoats. Again that old adage kicked in and since I had watched my Uncle Harry castrate hogs many times as a kid I decided to do it myself. It's not necessary to try to describe the wrestling match me and that shoat had, but I can assure you that he paid dearly for his un-co-operative attitude and he suffered considerable healing time of "butt" repair.

After living in our first home about seven years we decided to sell out and have a bigger home but realized that our house had very little curb appeal. In fact, to be honest it simply looked like what it really was "a patch on patch" novice attempt. But that could all be remedied by adding a carport, ripping off roof structures and rebuild with a new low-pitch roof over a car-port and house. This roof was the latest "California" look of white gravel and low pitch.

I had become infatuated with my carpentry skills and precut all the new roof rafters, stacked the sheeting and roll roofing handily in place before starting the tear-off. It was summertime August and I had listened to the radio several days before the planned week-end re-roofing. All reports were encouraging as to the possibility of rain, however I felt safer after investing in a plastic canvas just in case.

I was working the job by myself so I got out of bed before day break and began tearing off the roofs. Everything was going pretty well until about noon. The sky had been crystal clear when slowly a white cloud came floating in from the west about the size of Mittler Acres homing in on my project with rain coming out of it. I began scrambling around on the exposed ceiling joists trying to spread the plastic but slipped and stepped right through the kitchen ceiling. It rained on my project for about 15 minutes and then proceeded to move on across the Missouri river. There were no further clouds the rest of the day and I was able to finish the roof except for the white gravel application. Repairing and repainting considerable ceiling water stains in the following weeks were made thanks to that little rain cloud.

Self-taught lessons in-finance-home building - carpentry- veterinarian –heating-and more the hard way has infatuated me many more times I suppose.

Rambit and Rambet

This is probably the best point in this writing to explain a lifetime symbol of attraction that began in high school. My senior year consisted of a heavy load of makeup classes in order to graduate with the rest of my class. The previous three years were frittered away due to several circumstances, but mostly my infatuation with having fun. WW2 had been in full swing and every able bodied adult had been called upon to help with the war effort. I was working most of the evenings and skipping school quite a bit. My best buddy had obtained a pad of excuse forms that were supposed to be written by the office clerk stating missed work could be made up at the discretion of the teachers. We wrote our own excuses, not only were we having fun, but we were able to get away with what we considered managing our life activity. For anyone who did not live during those times, it may seem impossible that we were able to get away with something like this, but it should be remembered that everything was being rationed or in short supply, even paper.

Fortunately, since I had met Betty and managed to impress her with my dreams and ambitions. I became involved with a whole different set of friends, since I now had a steady girl-friend it occurred to me that I should make an effort to graduate with my classmates as an indication of worthiness. Since we had no classes together, I was only able to see her briefly in the hallway at class changes so it became necessary to pass little notes. I developed a face line drawing that looked somewhat like a little smirking rabbit with pursed lips and a pair of antenna. Since the drawing was intended to represent me, it was portrayed with a boy shirt collar and labeled Rambit. My initials being RAM and he was sort of an offshoot of a rabbit, I simply changed the "I" to an "E", again making an effort to impress her with my creativeness she became Rambet.

That little Rambit has stayed with us over the years. I must confess, I used his charming smirk by creating the girl Rambet facing him with the same pursed lips close to each other and hearts floating all around. Betty, still impressed with this creativity insisted that our grave marker be adorned with these characters.

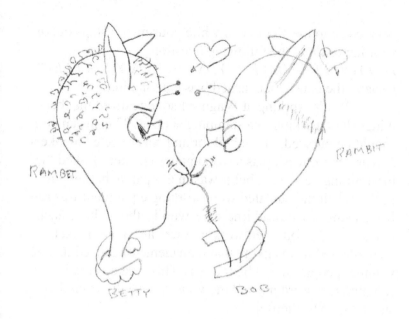

RAMBET

RAMBIT

BETTY

BOB

Job Horseplay Stories

My first job in the smoke stack industry was at
Wagner Electric in St. Louis Mo. My job description was
"stacker" which involved placing metal electric motor
stampings over a rotating shaft with a rib on one side. This
process prepared the proper quantity of stamped metal parts
for further development of a rotor for an electric motor. The
work was in a large building containing probably 100 punch
presses of sizes from small to huge. The noise in that
building was thunderous constantly and there were literally
tons of small pea size slugs of metal scrap every-where.

In order to hear it was necessary to put your mouth
next to some-one's ear and shout. A favorite trick to play on
a "new-be" consisted of holding a big handful of metal slugs,

walk close to the victim and while pouring the slugs out of your hand, shout the following question.
DID YOU EVER HAVE ANYONE PEE ON YOUR FEET?
Usually the dance that ensued was entertaining.

While working at Wagner I soon realized that better things than working in a stamping shop at .82 cents an hour should be pursued. I applied for and was selected to take a 3-year apprenticeship as a wood pattern maker. I liked the job-training very well, but it was in a separate building to itself and all the outdated woodworking equipment was run from a single overhead line shaft with leather belts to each machine. The four men working there as pattern makers were old and it was likely that management realized that new younger people should be trained. This created certain resentment toward me and my youth especially from the supervisor Mr. Steiffel.

My training for the first year was to unload and stack all the mill cut lumber, shovel the sawdust and keep the stinky hide-glue pots filled. Mr. Steiffel was a very tall German man with a heavy accent and after some time he began to let me saw cut and plane some of the simple dimensional wood blocks that were to be eventually hand carved into patterns by a Pattern maker.

His word was law and you dared not challenge it. He always insisted that I let him check the first piece for size, and his favorite method to get my attention was to stand on a big toe of my foot while he intentionally measured oversize. Then he insisted that I re-cut some off, which of course would then make the piece undersize. All this was done while addressing me as Dumkoff kid. I soon learned to ask one of the other pattern makers to verify my work.

Shortly after I joined pattern making the company started a long overdue job safety program and each department was required to have a Safety man. I volunteered for the job since the four pattern makers resisted change and I felt this might be an opportunity to advance into management. It didn't take me much more than one or two safety reports to get the overdue respect of Mr. hardnosed Steiffel.

Betty and I got married while I was still working at Wagner but ambition and low pay made me seek employment elsewhere. I found a job at a small company that was operating in receiver ship while continuing to manufacture fractional HP electric motors, household steam irons and window fans. The Bonding Company who was furnishing operating cash was looking for a Bonded Warehouse Agent to issue manufacturing raw materials on paid and approved requisitions as needed. I will never know how they were able to get me bonded since I was only 19 years old, but this gave me a certain feeling of importance after the hardnosed Steifel experience. I dropped several hints to persons still working at Wagner in hopes that old hard-nose would hear about my important job.   Being married was expensive and I was paid $37.50 week as a Warehouse Agent so I accepted another job in an aluminum casting foundry operating in the basement of the same building. This job consisted of breaking open sand molds that had been cast the day before and were solidifying and cooling. The job started at 2:30 AM and since I was the warehouse agent for upstairs I had a key to let myself in.

The molds were lined up in a row on the floor. Above them was a rail that held a riddling basket into which I was required to shovel the hot molding sand. This riddler served as a sieve to retain slag and aluminum scraps in order to prepare riddled molding sand for the day shift molders. I was to be paid $4.00 a night and every-thing went fine until the rows of sand began to grow longer and longer. The job was not supposed to take more than two or three hours which would give me time to return home for a shower and dress in clean clothes for my important job as Bonded Warehouse Agent. When the rows of sand grew to three or more I couldn't finish and was fired. I was glad because a couple of times I had no time for a shower before starting time for my other job.

Another Job Horseplay Story

I found a job in the wood shop at a railroad car company (ACF) American Car & Foundry making wood templates and wood hydro-form blocks for making aircraft components. The work and pay was better, since the company had obtained a military B47 bomber aft fuselage "section 43" subcontract. Fairly soon I secured a promotion job as a lofts-man in the aircraft components layout section. This job required us to work standing on a raised platform about three feet off the floor. Since the drawings were too large to be worked flat so they were positioned on a vertical table.

A fellow worker (big joker type) was given the job of painting the work platform legs while we were doing our work with our backs turned to him. From the corner of my eye, I watched him carefully brush paint the shoe heels of another lofts-man and I knew he was determined to paint me next. Just as he reached toward my heel with the paintbrush I quickly stepped backward on the paintbrush handle (feigning a necessary move) but pinching his fingers between the brush and the floor. I didn't let up on his fingers until I had satisfactorily heard a low moan of discomfort.

I eventually moved into and out of several jobs as a Process and Tooling Engineer working sixty or more hours weekly in various job-shops.

Sobering Effect

One of my best friends (Earl) and I, in our twenties, were avid fishermen and part-time students at Washington University had established as "almost sacred" Sunday morning as fishing time.   In our area (in order to go fishing) it was necessary to travel several miles to find a fishing spot. Earl also played drums in a local dance band and some-times my wife and I would accompany his wife to a local nightspot while he played music. One Saturday night we were all in a partying mood at one of our favorite places. We had a good time and closed the place officially several hours after the band had stopped playing. We danced to the jukebox and drank joy-juice with some other party monsters.

The gals drove us home to his house and as we pulled in his drive, lo and behold there sat in his driveway a fishing boat.   He and I "reasoned" that since it was Sunday morning, that boat must be put to use. The girls disgustedly went to bed while he and I packed gear, outboard motor and etc. into the fishing boat and started out for a day of fishing when the sun came up. Never did it occur to us that we were slightly influenced and had no sleep for twenty some hours. The small river we decided to fish was a pretty good river to troll and there was a good spot where we could leave the car.

Both of us still feeling joy-juice, as we piled in the boat for a trip upstream a few miles. I was sitting in the middle of the boat and Earl was running the motor as we were slowly making our way up stream. The early morning hours before day light created a foggy blanket about two or three feet thick hanging right on the water's surface.

Weird noises of all the landlocked creatures of the darkness surrounded us as they were finishing the night of ghoulish activity if you were prone to imagine creepy situations. But we were safe and sound in the water and every-one knows those creatures don't like water or the daylight soon to come, but it was fun to create spooky thoughts.

The boating was a slow process and we needed sleep and in fact I was nodding off when Earl tapped me on the back. He whispered to me in a very excited manner *"did you see that"* while pointing wide eyed up stream. I looked where he was pointing as the fog undulated higher and lower but I couldn't see a thing except fog and eerie daylight through the treetops.

I started to retire back to my restful ride when all at once Earl said, *"what the hell is that"*. This time I saw what had him spooked. Sweat and cold chills started up my spine as I began to think of escape from what I saw. Almost directly in front of us and descending silently upon us in the fog were **three huge mice with orange bodies accompanied by a large keeper with sticks in hand.**

Earl immediately (if not sooner) beached our fishing boat to the nearest bank, cut the motor, and tied up to the nearest tree root. We were trapped in our boat but took cover under the overhanging tree limbs. We watched breathlessly as the apparition slowly and silently descended upon us. The fog under the tree seemed to engulf us. The harder we breathed, the more convinced that we were near our last days on this earth. I knew the joy-juice I had been drinking was powerful stuff but never had I been subjected to hallucinations. As my spine tingled and the hair on my neck and arms stood on end the **huge orange mice in the fog came closer and closer**.

The monster mice were giggling almost ghoulishly among themselves no doubt gleeful with their prospective prey. Suddenly I realized that what we were looking at, was a family man in a rowboat and his three small children

wearing safety orange life preservers and Mickey Mouse
caps with the big black ears.
Never (well almost never) did I ever drink joy-juice again.

Frightful Experience

During the early "50's" I decided that every man should learn to fly an airplane. I contacted a small airport just north of St. Charles MO and was introduced to an instructor who encouraged me to fly at least twice a week. His airplane was a Piper Cub, 85 HP with a tail dragger landing gear and was likely to be twice my age. It was a fabric covered hi-wing craft with a control stick between my legs and seating fore and aft for two. There were four basic instruments altimeter, compass, turn-n-bank indicator and air speed gauge. After having completed a few hours my instructor informed me that I needed some flight simulator time in order to familiarize me with cross country flight procedures.

The simulator was located at his home and I was set up for a 9:00 am appointment. I prepared a flight plan and climbed into the simulator, complete with headphones and mock radio setup. After obtaining flight permission from the mock tower, I was under way in a closed dark canopy, lighted instruments and simulated engine noise. I had climbed to several thousand feet when I needed to change heading for my next check point.

As I moved the stick and pressured the rudder foot petal, I heard something snap. I began a steep downward spiraling dive and all the instruments began to spin and redline. I was unable to get any control over the simulator and soon found myself listing helplessly to the left and spinning round and round at less than sea level.

Unknowingly to me the instructor had decided to go for breakfast just after my take-off and it was about 20 minutes of listless spinning for me before he returned. He cut the power and unlatched the cockpit cover and jokingly informed me that I had died about twenty minutes ago due to equipment failure. While this was only a simulation it never the less gave me food for thought about pre-check procedures before taking off.

I put in several more hours with a live instructor and was finally OK'ed for solo flight time. No more simulated death crashes thank goodness.

I was excited to be flying alone and was told not to fly too far away from the airfield. Just go up to about four thousand feet and practice various maneuvers including some power-on stalls. So after about half an hour of time I decided that it was time to try a power-on stall. I opened the throttle completely and pulled the stick back against my belly. What an exhilarating thrill to hear and feel the fabric skin pulsing and the surging of the engine trying to pull me straight up into the air. Eventually gravity was overpowering all the little 85 horses as the craft was trying to hang on its propeller.

The plane fell off to the left and suddenly I was caught up in a power-on dive since I had failed to cut the throttle. Excitement and confusion engulfed me and suddenly I could see the conflux of the Missouri and Mississippi rivers coming up at me as the air-speed indicator was showing red line condition. Now the fabric was screaming at me as I was losing altitude fast and the altimeter was losing numbers. At some point I finally let go of the stick, cut the throttle and that forgiving little plane leveled itself out without any help from my inept hands. God and I never divulged the incident to my instructor but the sight of those rivers coming up at me has remained in my mind's eye to this day.

Fishing Fools

In the early 1950's, I was working as a tool Design Engineer at one of the many "job shops" in St. Louis Mo. Our federal government was spending big bucks on military aircraft since the Russians were no longer our friends and we were at the "top of the heap" economically and militarily. Work weeks were 40 plus 20 and Government money was no object when it came to maintaining our world position. This true story is primarily dedicated to the characters outlined and the enticing powers of office planning as an escape from the drudgeries of 60-hour work weeks.

Bob, the Bumbler and narrator on my 78th birthday
Gene, the German self-appointed Commander
Bruno, the Italian pitiful friend of the Commander
Don, the good natured Swede
Orville, the redneck homesick escapee

Anyway, three of my fellow engineers decided that a four-day fishing and camping trip to the further-most wilderness in Arkansas would refresh our worn out souls. One of the guys (Gene) was an officer in the Army reserves and **_HE_** decided to plan and lead the rest of us greenhorn "recruits". At least a month of planning and gathering of the necessities for this "bivouac" was a daily topic of office talk. Having never been subjected to the "Army" method of doing things, I began to suspect less than comfort since the "officer in charge" had borrowed back packing gear and each of us was expected to shoulder 50 to 70 lbs. of necessities according to his plans. We were to add whatever personal gear that we felt necessary for our own comfort. His plan for the "wilds" of Arkansas included ropes for mountain climbing, pistols to protect us from the razor back hogs, flares for emergency detection and many compass's, flashlights and field glass's.

Sleeping arrangements were up to our own choices and I teamed with Don Jensen for a two-man pup tent. The "German officer" Gene, teamed with his Italian buddy Bruno with a full blown 10 x 10 Artic comfort "home away from home" tent which Bruno had to put into his back pack. Late July being mostly hot and humid would not be too bad if they opened the window flaps on each side was Gene's reasoning to keep cool in the night if needed.

The "officer" had his back pack loaded with cooking gear which included a cast iron skillet and lid, since he had informed us that he was doing the cooking. Foodstuffs' consisted of several cans, some of which were brown in color and shaped like the sardine cans which Bruno had insisted on. Also was cornmeal, flour, salt and of all things a dozen eggs in a pressed cardboard carton and wrapped in a blanket. This was to be carefully placed on top of a back pack for obvious reasons. Two six-packs were to be included since a celebration was deserved after our first great harvest of the fish we were sure to catch.

We had a practice gear inspection meeting the weekend before departure date at which time we loaded all backpacks into a small tow-behind trailer. It was at this "beer and plan" session that the question *(where, in Arkansas are we going?)*. Our self appointed Commander in charge said *(don't worry, I have a friend Orville, from Arkansas that will be going along and he knows the area all around Jackass mountain)*.

Something told me to listen to my intuition and just put in for overtime for that weekend, but I didn't. Departure day came and that's when we met the hand picked guide and scout "Orville". His gear consisted of one Army blanket for bedding, one fishing pole with a hook attached, sun glasses, shorts and tennis shoes. His comment about not needing much, if you knew how to survive in the wild was a little irritating.

Five guys piled into the two door sedan driven by the Commander at about three in the afternoon which I suspicion-ed was a little late to be starting out since the drive was at least 8 hours. But the guide (seated in the front passenger side) assured us that he had lived there as a kid and it was wise to climb Jackass mountain in the cool of the night to get to the other side where a pristine clear water stream was located. He also assured us that this stream probably hadn't seen a human being since he was a kid. The car was black, the sun was bright, open windows nearly blew us out of the back, since air conditioning was still to become standard equipment, but thankfully the sun finally went down. We left the hi-way just before mid-night and drove many miles on gravel until our guide said "hesitatingly" *(pull off and park behind that old barn, I know who lives here and we will just leave a note on the car).* Jackass Mountain would soon be our home for the next few days.

Anticipation and quiet night air refreshed my expectations since I could see the mountain in the moonlight and the back pack was not really very heavy. Besides it was good to be out of that crowded back seat, squeezed between Bruno and Don. Our guide chose the very center of the mountain as our path of approach (claiming that the moon position was proper with the crest) and it was twice as far to go around in the valley. It was about 2 miles across hills of scrub oak and loose stone before we finally arrived at the foot of the mountain. The night air had turned exceptionally humid and the mosquitoes were tremendously pleased with our laboring breath and sweat. We continuously replenished our exposed skin areas with repellant. Our guide had given up on the moon for guidance by now and had picked a star in line with the crest of the mountain. My suspicions escalated of his navigation skills.

Now for the climb! Our Commanding Officer designated Don as our lead climber since he had obediently brought a couple hundred feet of hemp hay mow rope. His instructions were to tie off when an insurmountable table rock slab was encountered so the rest of us could "hand over hand" if need be. Bruno and I were instructed to hang Don's back pack on a pole and each of us would shoulder an end. Our Guide and Commander were to follow behind Don and cut branches if necessary for Bruno and I. Our ascent plan was now in place and we had only used a couple of night time hours, we were assured that we would arrive at the virgin trout stream in time for a morning breakfast catch. Now understand that an Arkansas mountain is not the same as you would expect in the Appellations' or the Rockies. Jackass Mountain was probably 900 feet tall and at least 45 degree slopes covered with alternating shelf stone and Cedar of the vicious variety. It turned out that as we ascended thru cedar thickets and over shelves of rock we would come upon a patch of pines that were considerably more friendly to climbers face and arms, but very unsympathetic to feet and knees. The pines had deposited several inches of past years needles on the slope and was as slick as grease to climb on.

After three more torturous hours we finally reached the top and another heavy decision was to be made by our leaders. It was still dark and the moon had long ago abandoned them, *so which way were we supposed to descend to fishing paradise.* Some very faint night time light was off to the right which indicated (according to Gene's deduction) east and that's where the sun usually comes up, so we started downward to the north. An argument had ensued between the Commander and the Guide about that light since the Guide believed the light was left over from the sun's rays from the day before. So, we were probably going south even though the stream was traveling north as he remembered from his childhood days. At this point I really didn't care which way was north.

Don was given his backpack since we hadn't encountered any table rock precipice situations on the way up and besides going down is always easier according to our Commander. That turned out to be another misguided opinion since a blanket of slick pine needles made it impossible to stay erect except to hang onto something. Our knees and ankles were now overworked in the pesky pine blanket and our back side's were under full attack. Commander Gene slipped at one place and rolled into our guide ahead of him smashing some of the eggs, which was not discovered until later.

Another hour was consumed until we could hear our precious fishing stream gurgling to us just ahead. Our steps (actually slides) hastened but were abruptly halted because we found ourselves atop a vertical wall of rock formation with our stream 20 feet below. Now another top command decision had to be made, go left or go right and it better be correct because those pesky pine needles would love to dump us over the side into the stream below. The decision to turn left was made with the rational that all streams head watered in the north or west. The waters will get shallower as we travel this direction since tributaries add water as a stream travels south. We spent another hour and finally found a spot where we could wade across in ankle deep waters to a sand bar just visible on the other side.

<u>Home at last,</u> but the stream was only about eight feet wide. Our guide assured us that this was not what he

had remembered as a young boy and with the coming of daylight he would be happy to locate the main stream since this was undoubtedly only a tributary. Anxious to begin the fun, I plopped my gear on the sandbar and broke out my fly rod since daylight was barely beginning to show. I was immediately chastised by the Commander for not preparing campsite accommodations, but I chose to ignore orders and pursue the intentions of this trip.

I had decided to move down stream until I could come upon the main river our guide had reassuringly told us was there. My hi-top leather mountain climbing (work shoe) boots were already soaked from fording the creek earlier, so I didn't bother to break out my rubber waders. Our guide had advised us (only thing I remember him being correct about) that the area was plentifully inhabited with snakes. I still had my 22-caliber pistol (loaded with birdshot) in the shoulder holster, so I had little fear of an attack

I could spend the next twenty paragraphs relating my next four hours of expedition miseries masqueraded as a fishing trip on an eight -foot-wide ankle deep creek with an occasional pool nearly three-foot-deep, sometimes inhabited by slant eyed water moccasin snakes. It's time for you the reader to forget about fish and concentrate on characters.

Meanwhile, back in temporary camp the officer in charge allowed the remaining group to relax against their back packs until daylight, but since Orville had only packed a blanket and a fishing pole, he immediately commandeered Bruno's folding beach chair which suffered some damage. This started a continuing dislike for Orville's brashness which our commander was forced to monitor for the remainder of the expedition. Don told me that daylight camp duties were dispensed almost as soon as I was out of sight. The first and most important task was for everyone to gather fire wood (even though it was the month of July). Bruno and

Don were instructed to chop into manageable lengths a few of the logs discovered a few hundred yards from the gravel bar encampment site. Each of them was equipped with hand axe's but the "Commander selected" log was hard oak, meanwhile Orville had taken on the duty of gathering kindling wood, which he claimed would allow Gene to heat his skillet quickly for pancakes.

It seems that Gene had packed ingredients for this, but had failed to bring along a mixing bowl, he also discovered the broken eggs and his egg soaked blanket. Don had brought along a two-quart thermos bottle for water and Gene decided that it could be used as a pancake mixer container provided all the ingredients were carefully loaded and the guys could take turns shaking the bottle while he prepared the skillet. This worked only in theory for the first pancake, but not after Don's water had been confiscated and the bottle was contaminated with flour. Gene then remembered that he had a bowl-shaped lid for his iron skillet that could serve as a mixing bowl. This incident, infused into the mind of Don, that maybe the Commander was not really as efficiently qualified as he had led us to believe. He had assured us back in the office that his responsibilities' in the army were in the food section, but it was discovered (by cautious questioning) his actual duties consisted of guarding supplies from pilferage.

With the coming of daylight and the refusal of a couple of ill-fed "recruits" to continue to cut fire wood logs, Commander Gene began directing the placement of temporary camp quarters. He was certain that a search team should be selected to explore the area for the actual roaring clear-water stream described to us back in town and that's where permanent (three days, two nights) camp should be built. In the mean-time even a temporary camp must be properly arranged in case of an attack by razor back hogs known to inhabit the wilderness. This meant that food supplies must be suspended in tree limbs, even the two six, packs Orville had conned him into. A search team consisting of Bruno and Orville (bad choice) was sent to locate the lost stream. Don was assigned the task of fishing the stream in the opposite direction that I had taken to procure the next meal of fresh fish. Don was happy to be relieved of camp building duties and found a comfortable spot just out of sight to relax and get some much needed rest. The morning sun was beautiful and the quiet atmosphere lulled him into a nice snooze until about 9:30 when Orville discovered him and his Snickers candy wrappers lying on the grass.

It seems that Orville had lost Bruno somewhere in the woods and he was not particularly concerned since Bruno had voiced his displeasure about the broken beach chair. Don and Orville continued to loaf in the woods for some time longer until the peacefulness was disturbed by six powerful gunshots rattled the air. Bruno was a city born and bred guy who had brought along his 45-caliber hand gun in case of hog or snake attacks. Having wandered aimlessly for the last hour he had become very concerned with the absence of humanity and decided to try to attract some attention. Sure enough he was only on the other side of the hill from temporary base camp when Commander Gene rescued him. Gene later disclosed his approach to Bruno was preceded with adequate whistles and shouts for fear that he might reload his gun and dispense with the approaching predator.

It seems that Gene had every right to be extra cautious about approaching Bruno and firearms since the winter before Bruno had peppered Gene's legs with buckshot while the two were rabbit hunting. Gene had driven his stick-shift to the hunting sight and due to his legs being shot he had to depend on Bruno to drive him to medical attention. Bruno was not familiar with anything other than an automatic transmission and the trip for medical attention was made with the car in low gear. They had remained friends anyway since Bruno always explained his mistake *"Why you no see me when I shoot"*.

The four of them returned to camp and received considerable lecturing about disturbances and lack of enthusiasm for duties associated with good times. I heard the shots, but delayed a return since I was pretty sure the shots were straight up in the air. I was pretty sure it was Bruno since he had requested Gene too allow him to carry one of the flares in case he got separated from us. Gene had wisely refused this since he was sure that a forest fire would ensue if Bruno should get separated from the group. I missed fish lunch back at camp and so did the others since Don hadn't caught a thing. Lunch consisted of more pancakes, but with a little more substance, due to the inadvertent addition of creek sand that was used by Orville to clean out the breakfast utensil.

I returned to temporary base camp around noon and since lunch was over, I scrounged into my backpack and located a stash of chocolate bars. I had placed my backpack on the gravel bar before the light of day and nobody had bothered to move it to shade. The heat from the sun had pretty much destroyed the firmness and I was relegated to lick the papers clean. I was careful to keep my stash hidden as much as possible since I had noticed Orville watching and something told me caution was wisdom.

Gene had decided that since no one had located the stream, we should start making more permanent campsite accommodations. His 10x10 tent was placed on the gravel bar a few feet from the stream. After he and Bruno struggled to drive stakes and erect the tie ropes, Orville casually mentioned that he remembered the river had overflowed its banks many times when he was a kid. Bruno immediately began to worry that this could happen instantaneously and we were all in dire danger of a flash flood and could probably be separated from our vehicle and civilization. Orville seemed to enjoy adding more to this situation until Gene had to shut him up. Bruno complained over and over until Gene decided that we should move camp back on the uphill side of the creek.

All gear had to be moved back through the water where level ground was nearly nonexistent. Don and I located a small swale in the hillside pretty much filled with pine needles. We set up our two-man pup tent over this which made a comfortable bed, however the sides tended to tip us to the center but we felt we could deal with this by placing a small log between us. Everyone replenished our insect repellant on exposed skin and even shared our supplies with Orville since he hadn't brought any for himself. Poor Gene and Bruno were unable to drive stakes into this since it was basically shallow soil over rock. They were confronted with tying off the support lines to as many scrub oak trees as they could locate. The shape of their home was less than it was designed to be and you could say that the results were more in keeping with a large blanket with a floor and an un-shapely roof. However, they each had air mattress sleeping bags which caused some amount of envy in the group. Orville chose to spread his army Blanket out on a flat sheet of shelf rock claiming that his heritage had well prepared him for less than comfort in the wilds. There was little envy in the rest of us for his approach to rustic accommodations.

Evening time was upon us sooner than we had expected since remaking camp had been tedious. All foods had to be removed from the trees in the first campsite and relocated into new tree locations on our new site. Large trees other than evergreen varieties were scarce and leaving food in some of the trees on the other side meant that we would have to cross thru water anytime we wanted something. Our evening meal turned out to be gourmet since Gene had brought along some packages of hot dogs and a small jar of mustard. However, the iron skillet, properly rinsed this time, could only accommodate a few of the hotdogs at a time, this meant that one hotdog each was available at a serving with only one left over. The skillet was filled with creek water for the preparation of boiled hot dog dinner and Gene had thoughtfully saved some pancakes from lunch to be used for buns. (Orville volunteered to eat the extra hot dog much to our chagrin, if the rest of us didn't mind too much.) Bruno began to protest loudly at the absence of bread, but shut up after Gene threatened to deny him one of the beers in the six-pack. (Orville had already discovered the creek style beer fridge.) Don and I decided to consume our second hot dog straight from the package since the skillet water was now sort of black from burning kindling sparks and leaves. Some small cans of pork & beans were heated near the fire but also suffered some of the same contaminates that the skillet water had seen. Don and I ate from the same can set on the ground since it had burned Don's fingers. Gene had administered considerable medical treatment from his back pack, explaining that he had once intended to become a doctor of medicine, but felt his contribution to society would be just as meaningful in the country's defense industry. Twinkies were produced as desert, thanks to wrappings, the only part of the evening meal that represented clean and enticing dining, although I wasn't sure about the cleanliness of our hands since finger food was the fare of the evening.

Nightfall descended on us rather early since we had little rest in the last 24 hours and we each turned in for the night. Orville lay his body out on his flat rock bed first, and made a few comments about sleeping sound while being lulled by the gurgling waters just below. The rest of us retreated to our respective accommodations not really believing him, but satisfied that we had made proper plans for our own comfort. Don and I soon decided that tomorrow we would search for a larger separating pole and one that had fewer protrusions. Gene and Bruno retreated to their "chateau" and were having difficulties blowing up the air mattresses due to a collapsed roof over them, but the rest of us wasted little sympathy on them and their superior comfort plans. Considerable pre-sleep conversations eventually subsided and the camp became silent.

Shortly after this Orville began arousing the rest of the camp by asking us to help him gather some pine needles for a mattress on his flat rock bed We had little sympathy for him and it was only after Commander Gene requested we help him that some suggestions were made. He refused to simply move to a pine needle covered spot on the ground since the moisture would soon soak his blanket. So with much complaining we began to gather bedding material in the dark for him. Orville asked if one of us would loan him a backpack to be used as a pillow for his head at which time Bruno volunteered his broken beach chair and again Gene had to intercede. He finally obtained Don's backpack for a pillow, but soon complained again that it was stinky. Don being a practical guy had bought some fish bait to use since he had no intentions to be a purest depending on artificial lures. Part of his fish bait was still in his backpack and it had been cooked by the sun all day long. Don begrudgingly got out of bed and removed the fish bait to satisfy Orville's sensitive nose.

The camp then re-settled into the night-ness for some well-deserved rest, but it was only for a short while until

Bruno was heard to loudly chastise his bunk mate. It seemed the beans and weenies had taken over Gene's resistance. The tent had been securely zipped even in its collapsed condition and Bruno was struggling to extricate himself in the darkness. Meantime he was screaming *Why you no respect me from your filthy body? You krauts are aint humans! Where I be spending tonight? I think you be spend night on rock with hillbilly.* Gene was angered with this attack on his heritage and responded *You wapps couldn't even walk on your hind legs until we invented the wheelbarrow.* Don and I realized this needed some cool interference and found ourselves trying to appease the other three. A negotiated peace plan consisted of Bruno being placed with his face close to the un-zippered opening so that he could breathe night air here in paradise, but extra insect repellant had to be applied for the mosquitoes.

The rest of the night went almost without incident until a slow misty rainfall started in the early hours of the morning. With this Orville was awakened to not only the gurgle of the fresh water stream but also the dropping of rain on that water. He immediately insisted on occupancy with Gene and Bruno which was not a happy circumstance for the chateau dwellers. Don and I snickered between ourselves and swore to be friends forever as long as we shared a two-man pup tent with an appropriate dividing pole.

Early morning came much later than it should have since misery of many sorts had befallen our little expedition into fishing paradise. Don and I both wanted to make the best of the situation and decided to arise and search downstream together for the elusive big stream full of fish. We left camp with fishing gear in hand as well as some of Don's stinky bait, while the other three were holed up in a collapsing tent and drizzling rain. After a mile or two traveling downstream we came to a fork in the stream which consisted of a much smaller stream than our eight foot wide one. We determined that our stream was undoubtedly the one that our guide had in mind when he loosed us on Jackass Mountain which was now considerably behind us. We hadn't stopped to fish yet since none of the pools were big enough to house anything bigger than crawdads or minnows. Neither of us would admit discouragement even though we were soaked from head to "water logged" feet. The stream, however did seem to get a slight amount bigger or maybe our mutual hopes were erasing reality. Now that the stream was getting bigger it was determined that it would be expedient for us to separate and travel one on each side and if a pool of water was discovered we could attack from two sides for a really big kill. This was a very good and workable plan, however the underbrush was pretty thick in places and we would lose sight of each other occasionally. It was decided that we should whistle from time to time so each of us could know where the other one was at that moment. This worked fairly well for the next hour or so but we really hadn't come upon any great amounts of water, however I did come upon a small hole about three times as large as anything else I had seen. I decided to cast into it a few times and wait for Don to approach on the other side especially since he hadn't returned my whistle the last couple of times. I fished the hole for maybe 20 minutes and caught a monster Pickerel about eleven inches long. My reasoning at the time was that if we ate him along with the other fish we were bound to catch, no great harm would come from eating an illegal infant that was trapped in an environment that would stymie his growth into adulthood.

I began to think maybe Don was walking ahead of me, so I better give up and hurry ahead whistling continuously but I couldn't seem to catch up to him. The sun came up with a fierceness that only a Mississippi valley resident can appreciate after a summertime drizzle. The humidity was well into the ninety's percent and the day was starting toward the middle. My stomach reminded me that I had denied myself of the campsite pancakes, but I did have two wads of paper containing what used to be candy bars and were now blobs to be licked off the wrappers. I decided to turn back to camp now determined that Don had already given it up and returned to camp. It seemed that the return was much quicker and I arrived in camp about noon. Don wasn't there, but we all felt that he would soon show up. Besides, I removed my boots and discovered blisters on both feet since I had carelessly allowed water to over flow the tops a couple of times.

The rest of the group was not a bunch of happy campers and there was considerable talk of returning back over Jackass Mountain to the car and civilization. But what about Don! maybe lost out there? The last of the six packs had been consumed instead of lunch, but good old Gene had prepared for this eventuality. He offered me Army issue "C" rations and my education about Army workings were expanded. They all made fun of my great fish catch and I was tempted to attempt reviving him in the stream, but decided just to place him there on the chance that mother nature would take care of another of it's miserable creatures. Don finally showed up about 3:30 in the afternoon and related his encounter with wandering in what was a full circle three times before determining which way was camp. He had actually sat down at one point and fired several shots in the air, but he was only armed with 22 caliber short bullets and they only make about as much noise as a lady finger firecracker. The decision to return back to the car was made over the objections of myself and half-heartedly Gene who still had considerable food items mostly for fish cooking.

We packed all the (months long gathering) gear as quickly as possible in order to get underway before nightfall. We reached the top of Jackass Mountain at about dusk and off to our left was a considerable amount of light showing in the sky. An immediate argument ensued about the source of this light that seemed to get brighter as the evening progressed. Orville was convinced it was the sun going down and Commander Gene reasoned that it was of a manmade source. Anyway we just made sure it was always to our left and by this time Gene had broken out one of his compass's.

We arrived back at the car at about ten in the evening and were immediately confronted by the people that owned the property. Orville's acquaintances had long ago sold to the people now confronting us, having claimed not seeing a note. It seems that a recent amount of thievery was taking place in the neighborhood and the Constable had been working all afternoon trying to get information from Little Rock about the vehicle with a trailer to haul away stolen items. This system was considerably before the day of electronic information and all correspondence was handled by phone service if you had one. No amount of convincing by any of us could keep the property owner from sending his son down the road to the neighbor's phone and place the emergency call to the night Constable.

The delay in our departure was somewhat enlightening but extremely painful when we learned that a farm-to-market road had been built just about a half mile the other side of Jackass Mountain. We could have driven into the lighted town about four miles away and had restaurant food most anytime had we only known that the road existed only a short distance from our camp site. The Constable arrived and verified that the car belonged to a city slicker from St. Louis and casually mentioned something to the country folks about the lack of sense some folks had. We gave all the left over camping food to the property owners in exchange for some left over biscuits and milk which would get us into town for some genuine food and resting accommodations.

Lucky Goat

In the early 50s Betty and I had built our first house which was actually a 12' X 20' future garage according to our long range plan. We had bought a two-acre plot of land on contract in the country about three miles out of town. I had worked for the local lumber yard during high school which gave me the opportunity to obtain building materials on credit from Mr. Rauch. We paid every dime that we could earn to make land and lumber payments, and were slowly gaining equity worth. Our first son (Gary) was about 3 years old and being the first grandson for Betty's mother and Step father, he was endeared to a fault sometimes especially by his Grandpa Jones'ie.

Now Jones'ie was a hard-working man and also a hard drinking man, and when he was inebriated he could be especially entertaining to little children. One Saturday Betty and I were visiting, but Jones'ie had decided to attend an auction somewhere with one of his drinking buddies. Three young goats were put on the auction block and Jones'ie won the bid. His buddy promised to take one goat and grandpa decided that he would keep one and give the other one to his grandson. They proceeded to load the goats into his car and head for home. Upon arriving home, he entered the house and announced that he had made a very important purchase for his grandson and insisted upon taking him outside to see his new present. Of course our son Gary was thrilled beyond words with the prospect of having a goat play mate. I had been napping on the sofa when Betty aroused me and insisted that I go outside and see what "Jones'ie" had done.

I arrived at the car just in time to see my mother-in-law with hands on her hips extolling the virtues of married life upon Jones'ie while trying not to show too much disapproval for grandson's ears. My son Gary had been placed inside the car and was caressing his new goat friend that Grampa had given him. Betty and I both stammered objections to the gift, but to no avail since Grampa promised to bring the goat over to our house that day. Since we had little to none lawn equipment, we were told that the goat would be an asset by keeping grass and weeds down and besides you can't deny your son. So much for reasoning with a drunken hero adult and an admiring grandson!

The goat was tethered and given a doghouse at the back of our house just under the kitchen window. Betty and I were overwrought with the prospect of caring for an animal that was far outside our budget or time allocations. Sunday our son played with his new friend all day long and carefully locked him in the doghouse for the night. Monday was a workday for both of us and Gary was sent over to Grandma for babysitting where he played with Grampa's goat all that day.

I had opened the doghouse door and watered Gary's goat before heading off to work for the day. The goat was tethered on a chain about 10' long and had plenty of food and water. I returned home that afternoon and upon entering the house immediately sensed a problem. The goat had jumped upon the top of his doghouse, broken thru the kitchen window, jumped onto the kitchen sink breaking dishes and proceeded to jump off the countertop to the floor.

Luckily for the goat the chain was about two foot to short and he had hung himself. The damage to everything was extensive, but nothing compared had I been home to catch him in the act. Gary was told that his goat ran away and *"NO"* he couldn't have another goat.

Stubborn Dad

My Dad and Mom had bought a couple of acres just down the dead end road from where Betty and I had bought our first home sight. World war 11 had brought on a whole new economy and most every-one who wanted could be employed. This was the first time in his life he was a homeowner thanks to a new economy. Dad being a farm boy had fenced the back of his property which existed as a steep hillside that was nearly impossible to maintain. He had obtained a sow hog with the idea of raising some butchering stock to help feeding the remaining houseful of kids at home.

Since I lived close by, Dad had asked me to come over and help him one day with his brood sow. It had become nearly impossible to keep the sow inside the fenced area since she had nearly uprooted every-thing on this hillside pen. As anyone knows even a well fed hog will root around nearly all day looking for grubs, roots or anything else edible. A fence only makes the challenge more interesting and even fun to root under raise it overhead and walk away with a nice back scratch on the way.

The hog shelter was at the bottom of the hill and sometimes the sow would lie down there. In case you are not familiar with hog anatomy, they are blessed with a tough gristle appendage on the end of their nose forming a semicircle shape just over the mouth and blessed with a powerful neck and front legs for rooting the ground. Hog farmers many decades ago learned to pierce this appendage with metal rings using a pliers like tool for closing open rings in place on the gristle snout. These rings being nearly permanent would discourage rooting since it was uncomfortable like a bee sting when attempting to dig. Usually a couple of rings were sufficient but Dad's sow must have been pain resistant or plain stubborn since she would invariably continue to dig under the fence to freedom by digging sort of sideways where there were no snout rings.

Dad's patience was exhausted, so we were prepared to decorate her entire semicircle snout shape with rings. Now she was no dummy and the minute we approached her (with ropes in hand) at the bottom of the hill lying in her lair, her eyes and attitude became resistant to say the least. She would back into a corner of the fence and glare defiance while grunting a challenge. Dad was raised to be a good domestic animal handler so the plan was for me to get her attention with a bucket of corn while he would attempt to get at least one front leg and one back leg in a noose so she could not run.

Several attempts failed so Dad decided to simply grab two legs and throw her to the ground while hobbling her four legs (cowboy style). Now this hog weighed somewhere close to 300 lbs. at about three feet tall and probably a little disgusted with her two antagonist's. Dad managed to get a rope on her but it was only on a front leg as she began to run top speed up the hill <u>dragging</u> Dad no longer on his feet while hanging on to the rope in desperation. She made it to the top of the hill squealing and snorting the challenge. She turned around for a return trip downhill and Dad managed to get another loop on the two back legs, so over she went on her side kicking like a mule. Dad got up allowing loose plowed dirt and mud to dribble down inside his overalls. He then accused her heritage of being from canine evolution while he decorated her nose with as many rings as he could. He had lost a shirt, overall strap, shoe, watch, glasses and temperament but the rings discouraged her fencing habit. This incident should have educated me about swine handling but then that's another story about pigs and me.

Talcum Powdered Baby Boys

Being young married couples in the early fifties Clarice and Clarence (Hanebury) and us both had our first baby boys. We rented the upstairs apartment over an older homeowner couple in St. Charles Mo. We were close friends and visited each other often mostly to compare family experiences of our own since we already had a couple decades of parental family back ground experience. This particular evening, we were pretty much engrossed in big plans for the future as well as the joy and cares of our second newly born infant babies.

Since both our first born boys were nearly the same age of about three, they were pretty much conversation interrupters of which the two mothers became tired of occasionally. Since our son had a fair amount of little boy toys in the bedroom, the girls decided it would be expedient to allow the two boys to play in the bedroom with the door closed since their excessive Cowboy and Indian play was distracting.

We adults played cards and attended to our second baby infants as needed and I suppose quite a bit of time elapsed. The two bedroom boys had quieted down for some time before the two mothers decided to check on them. Upon opening the bedroom door, a frustrated outcry ensued and was heard by Clarence and me as we both dashed to see what kind of disaster must have taken place.

As we hurried from the kitchen into the living room the atmosphere distinctly smelled of baby powder. We quickly stepped to the open bed room where the odder increased considerably and discovered two wives literally wringing their hands in desperation upon discovering two young boys literally covered in white baby talcum powder. As well as the linoleum floor which we later decided had made a perfect slide. In addition to cleaning clothes and boys the room was never the same since a baby powder smell remained prevalent even after we moved out.

Painted Kids

In the 1950's, homemaker's generally decorated rooms with various colors of paint usually, bedrooms were pastel blue or pink. Betty and I had bought an unfinished home near St. Charles just off Friedens road. Having collected several partial cans of leftover paint I decided it was time to dispose of them. I had spent Sunday afternoon gathering paint cans and had opened some of them to determine whether they were worth saving. I owned an old Chevrolet pick-up truck and had loaded the bed with various items to be taken to a dumping place in a few days.

Our two oldest sons (about 5 & 3) were allowed to play in the bed of the old truck from time to time. Unbeknown to Betty, on the following Monday they had climbed into the truck bed and discovered some of the open paint cans. Since it was summertime they and the Stewart kids from next door, were playing in short pants and no shirts. They proceeded to paint themselves especially the legs and bellies, then having had enough fun with the paint they decided to play in the dirt and sand in the backyard. Sometime there-after Betty decided to check on them and was horrified to discover that they were not only painted various colors, but also caked with dried sand and dirt.

Now Betty is a very steady person when it comes to daunting situations, and I have always been a helpful husband when called upon, but this one was more than she could resolve without some expert help of removing sand paint from young bodies.

So she placed a long distance call to me at my workplace and apologetically requested of the secretary if I could be called to the phone for a minor problem at home. She must have indicated *"nothing serious, but our boys had gotten into some paint"* so when the secretary informed me of this, my warped sense of humor kicked in.

Betty explained the situation to me and wanted to know if I thought anything stronger than soap and water could be used. Foolishly, I quipped *"Just flush em down the toilet, it's easier to make new ones than to clean em up"*, **phone went dead.** The guys at the office thought it was a pretty good answer, however my additional family making was terminated for a long time afterward.

It took a long time but persistence pays.

Chapter Eleven:

Michigan's Luck

Dinner for Two

I had accepted a new job in Utica Michigan and had moved my family there. An early dinner allowed time for weekly grocery buying taking the two younger ones (Karen was not born yet) with us while the two older boys (14 & 12) were given the job of washing and drying the dinner dishes. We were living in a rented home until such time we could move into our new home under construction. Our oldest son Gary always an antagonistic teaser of his younger brother Danny but nonetheless essentially well behaved and responsible while his younger brother was responsible but quick tempered with a short fuse.

One payday after dinner we arrived home with the week's groceries. Upon entering the back porch just off the kitchen, we were stopped short before opening the door into the kitchen by the sound of our oldest son's taunting voice and his younger brother screaming at his antagonist. As I listened thru the closed door for a few seconds the confrontation escalated as the oldest whip cracked his brother's butt with a drying towel and quickly dashed into the bathroom just off the kitchen.

He closed the door behind him just in time to avoid a full dinner plate thrown on the door filled with table scraps. At this very moment, I opened the door and two young boys suddenly saw their lives pass before them. Mother entered and immediately began to attempt a mediation settlement, however I calmly instructed the boys to clean-up the broken china and food while I determined a fitting punishment.

After the clean-up including the rest of the dishes were silently and speedily finished I announced that punishment would be pronounced tomorrow after work. Next day (likely of high suffrages) just as we all sat down to our dinner plates I calmly removed one of the boy's dinner plate from the table announcing that for the next *two weeks* there would only be *one dinner plate for the two* of them. Death might have been sweeter than having to share food eaten from a brother's dinner plate.

New Home & Kids

It was the early sixties and we had recently moved into an upper-middle class neighborhood in Rochester Mi. We were committed to raising our kids in as fine a home environment as possible and keep up with the spit & polished look of the neighborhood. This sometimes presented considerable effort when you consider a house full of kid's corralled pretty much at home, while Betty & I worked hard at job responsibilities. For instance, our front yard was carpeted with Blue-Marion (instant beauty) grass, but it needed to be looked at more than walked on. Our choice was to let the kids play with their new friends in our front yard and suffer the consequences of any abuse to the pristine look expected by some of the neighbors.

I worked 6 days a week at my young man Executive job and had limited time available for lawn boy or maintenance man duties and Betty was busy raising infant daughters. The kid's regular front yard ball game activities and the irregular lawn care caused a few blemishes in the front lawn of our house such as a couple of brown spots and fairy rings. Since my time was pretty much spoken for, I was willing to over-look this until later. However, adding to the declining "looks" standard of the neighborhood according to the "looks patrol lady" somebody's baseball broke a pane of glass in the front garage window.

"T'wasen't me that did it" was the innocence plea heard over and over during the investigative process. It was necessary for me to go out of town for a few days, so the broken window remained in that condition for several days before I could get a measurement for a piece of replacement glass. Finally, I collected tools putty and new piece of glass for a Sunday replacement job. In the mean-time a few of the neighborhood "looks" patrol had made some well-placed comments about how the Miller house was beginning to degrade.

I started the glass job by chiseling all the broken glass and putty from the frame. I had the new piece of glass leaning against the wall at my side when my oldest son Gary joined me for what I suspect was a cover-up of some guilt. He was always the one for teasing and I was considered fair game I suppose. I nearly had the gaping opening prepared for new glass when he picked up the hammer and teasingly said "How close do you think I can hammer the wall near that piece of glass?"

I replied "Put the hammer down!" as he started tapping on the brick wall well above the new glass. But each little tap he made was lowered nearer and nearer the glass as he grinned and failed to hear my "desist & cease" command. As I reached for the hammer to disarm him he misjudged his next strike and broke the new glass.

It was fully another two weeks before I could get another glass, so the gaping hole on the front of the house provided more conversation I am sure. The tongue wagging of the "look's" patrol went into hi-gear, while Mom's corrective measures for the next week were initiated on our oldest playful son.

Memories of Daughters

Karen has always had vocal music appreciation, for instance when she was a tiny baby a sure way to get her to stop crying for no reason other than perhaps "getting attention" was to sing to her. Now I know this is not much different than other small babies, but Karen was very particular about the song. Her favorite was a song about some baboons going on a honeymoon or maybe it was monkeys getting married, but at any rate it was interspersed with "aba-daba-daba said the monkey to the chimp, aba-daba-daba in monkey talk means, means monk I love you too"—"said the big baboon, one night in June, he married them and very soon they went upon their aba-daba honeymoon". After this first line in reasonable tempo, she expected a repeat of the line but the tempo was to be much faster and then even faster yet until your tongue became twisted at which she would giggle and request more over and over.

After Karen became more mature (probably at least another year) her mother composed a new song which seemed to catch on since the lyrics were tailored around her name over and over. I don't recall the many verses, but the chorus was always "run Karen, run Karen run Karen run". The verses mostly consisted of "situations of excitement" that required her to depart into another interesting experience. Her mother seemed to have and endless storeroom of exciting things for a little girl to do.

As Karen became more acquainted with the world of vocal music, she decided to entertain herself and every-one else within earshot with her rendition of a popular song of the airwaves "Downtown", all during her waking hours she was almost chanting Downtown- downtown- downtown- downtown (boring, isn't it?) You should have been there since this is as many times as I intend to write it, but understand if this were Karen it would seemingly go forever or unless you gave her a fresh bottle of milk.

As Karen developed into a beautiful young teen-ager she participated in several musical renditions with her school friends. I would like to believe that she was destined for theatrical performances but, alas she discovered boys. Then after the fascination with boys passed she engaged in a more "young adult" pastime entertaining the drinking crowd's in the Karaoke bars.

As a responsible parent I feel the time has arrived to consider sponsoring my daughter's vocal talents at some accredited school of music, but then again maybe she'd just as soon keep her talents for her own personal enjoyment. Besides as time went by after this thought I decided that the bar-bill costs would be prohibitive, however time has blessed her with a beautiful voice.

Child's Persistence

Our oldest daughter was about three or four years old and she was obsessed with her oldest brother's pet obsession. He was always finding another varmint, creature, bug, bird or animal to bring in the house. Betty was as tolerant as she could possibly be with the aggravation of having to check the bedrooms on a regular basis to make sure that we weren't living with a strange creature or animal that didn't fit into the life style we had in mind.

One day our daughter (Jeannie) had been playing with a neighbor friend and discovered a mother kitty and litter of several youngsters. She asked the friend if she could have some of the kittens to take home and of course the answer was positively "yes", but she would need to wait until the kittens had grown up a little more. Jeannie came home and announced at the dinner table that she was going to get several kittens in a few days and immediately she received a very positive *"NO"*.

She put on her best positive expression and we parent's knew that the problem might not go away that easily. Sure enough the next few days were filled with pleading conversation about the nice little kittens that she could get in a few days. Betty and I stood our ground and put our best reasoning rejections to her, but the determination just seemed to build, especially after she visited with her kitten family to be. Jeannie pointed out to us that her older brother had pets and she should have the same rights. After several objections to her pleading, **she** finally decided that just one kitten would be enough.

We held our ground and gently but firmly rejected this because of all the care and keeping another animal would cause an already crowded situation. This reasoning didn't seem to make any difference to Jeannie's resolve. One morning as I was shaving in the bathroom, I heard Betty call me to "come here", and I could tell as only a husband can, that the call was for something urgent.

I slipped into some pajama bottoms and wearing shaving cream on my face, I could see Betty standing at the garage entryway door with a look of dismay on her face. As I approached, a pathetic little girl was standing in front of her mother squeezing a half grown kitten to her chest. The kitten's back legs were dangling and its eyes were wide open as if asking a question "wanna keep me". Jeannie had fetched this kitten early in the morning, up the street and was pleading pathetically to let her keep it.

All I could do was throw up my hands and say *"Oh hell-----* *"I GIVE UP"*

Leprechaun's Friend

When our daughter Jeannie was probably about three years old she had developed a little imaginary friend who accompanied her everyplace. We had no idea where she obtained this image, however she could describe him in great detail as a leprechaun. She could tell you how he was dressed or how tall he was and that he could talk or sing to her.

Since he was her continual companion, she would carry him around on her hand and was especially careful that he didn't get hurt or lost in the daily management of our house full of kids. There were times when her leprechaun advisor would disapprove of Mom's instructions or needs, and this would escalate into specific direction from the imperial authority.

A light discussion had taken place between Betty and I about the seriousness of the infatuation with this character and it was determined that it would simply go away someday. It is highly likely that an older brother had been privy to this conversation. One evening as we all gathered at the dinner table, Jeanie sat next to her older brother. She very carefully sat her leprechaun friend on the edge of her drinking glass of water and instructed him to be careful and wait for her to eat before going back out to play. Several times she was engrossed in conversation with the leprechaun which irritated her brother Daniel.

He asked her where this guy was and she showed him that he was sitting on the edge of her drinking glass. Big brother simply flicked the leprechaun into the water, stirred the water with his finger and laughed as Jeannie began to cry that he had drowned her friend. She cried herself into her room and far into the evening, for big brother was a villain for his actions.

We attempted to console her, about her loss and maybe he just took a bath and would soon be back, but nothing would work. She had lost her best friend forever and many days of mourning and consoling took place before she could face life alone again.

She still remembers in adult hood this incident.

Landscaping Help

Upon accepting a new job at a small metal working shop as Executive Vice President in the early sixty's, we moved into a new upper–middle class home in Rochester MI. Having been raised in mostly poor circumstances, I was never taught pretentiousness since we were pretty much relegated to the lower stratus of society. This likely set my personality profile for life, in addition to always looking for a laugh at my- self or others if possible.

Immediately upon moving into the neighborhood we were encouraged to join the Newcomers Club especially since the word had gotten out that I worked as a Vice President and my wife didn't have to work. Betty and I joined after thinking it would be kind of nice to make some new friends. The first encounter was a semi-formal dance, neither Betty nor I had been to a meeting before this social event came about so we were totally unprepared for who represented what in the organization.

Having finished a meal with some nice people, the dance music began and we danced together a couple of times. We have always been pretty fair dancers and the president of the club began to encourage all to trade dances with your neighbors to get acquainted. Our house happened to be located at the bottom of a small hill and the back yard was covered with virgin trees and a little creek at the back property line. We had no intention of landscaping the back since it was a perfect place for our kids to partake of mother nature's offering since everything behind us was open land and timber.

It was not very long before the self appointed neighborhood "looks" patrol lady just a few doors uphill from us approached me for a slow dance. I accepted having been forewarned of her tenacious information gathering techniques. Following is the transcription of that slow dance conversation as best I can recall:

Her: *I under-stand you are a Vice President.*

Me: *Yes*

Her: *Do you have options at your company?*

Me: *Yes* (She didn't ask what kind of options and I always figured I could option to quit)

Her: *I under-stand you fly the company airplane.*

Me. *Yes* (After the boss took off, turned on the auto pilot I could make heading changes)

Her: *You and "your, what's her name" wife have several children.*

Me: (becoming a little impatient since her concentration was not on her clumsy feet)

Me: *Yes! It's Betty, and we are going to make several more!*

Her: Stunned, she decided to probe another subject. *What city were you raised in?*

Me*: I wasn't raised in any city, I was raised on a farm. (I was tempted to say a reform school farm)*

Her*: Do you intend to landscape your big backyard this spring with grass and plantings?*

Me: No (becoming aggravated*) **As soon as I get the fence up, my Uncle is giving me some goats to help keep the weeds down.**
She stumbled slightly as she departed for her table and the next few weeks were filled with neighborhood gossip about those redneck "Millers" and the goat fence that was going to be put up.

Food Vending Entrepreneur

In the early sixties, having a job managing a small company doing mostly experimental work for some of the various research Laboratories and Universities around the country gave me exposure to an occasional entrepreneur. My job included entertaining business associates from time to time at lunch time at some of the better restaurants in the area. Having had several lunch's at one of these I became acquainted with a Stoufers Food manager who insisted that I assist him with the development of a vending machine business he and another person were developing. They anticipated installing vending machines in parking garages of high rise apartment complexes to vend dinners to the occupants.

The problem with the machines available from The Vendo Company was that only four choices could be offered from the machine as designed. Since having done previous product work at the Vendo company something convinced him that I could rework their first machine they had bought to offer greater choices of dinners. I tried in vain to refuse acceptance of the machine at my employer's shop since this was nowhere close to what we did.

I will never know how he found out my home address, but the vending machine was delivered there. A promise of one third of profits made would be mine when I redesigned and rebuilt the machine. This machine was about the size of a large home refrigerator and being challenged, I proceeded to develop drawings and modifications at home in the evenings. My redesign and rework was successful and they placed the machine in the Ann Arbor Towers parking garage. Many months went by and I never heard from either of the guys about the profits that were expected.

I had retained all my drawings for the redesign project and one day I decided to contact The Vendo Company about the project. I found out upon visiting them in Kansas City that they had confiscated the machine for non-payment, but agreed to a small compensatory amount for my drawings. I guess I had forgotten Aunt Hattie's teachings about dressed-up crooks, since I now dressed up for work every day.

Dog Poop Control

Living in a middle class (beer salary, champagne taste) neighborhood can some- times be tedious. We had lived in our new home about 5 years. The neighbor adjacent on the north had a much larger home than ours. In fact, he had most everything much larger than ours. His ego to start with, not to mention the new convertible, the eight kids and the biggest St. Bernard dog you can imagine. He held membership in some of the most frequently visited social drinking establishments in town.

This was likely a job-related requirement since he was marketing manager for a local manufacturing company. We rarely spoke, mostly because his arrival at home was much later than mine and his departure was usually in well-worn late morning hours.

But weekends were a little different since his favorite show for everyone to see consisted of setting his St. Bernard in the back seat of his topless yellow convertible and cruise a few times for the neighborhood to see a dyed in the wool egomaniac.

Now this really didn't bother me all that much, however the toiletry habits of his dog were a neighborhood problem. The dog seemed not to be prejudiced as far as which neighbor's yard he visited and left a collection that would put any self-respecting cow to shame. After being approached by most of the nearby neighbors including myself about the dog poop deposits, he would delegate one of his eight children to walk the dog. This was consistently a short-time fix and soon the old situation would begin all over. One neighbor actually moved a large deposit onto his front porch in an attempt to get the attention of Mr. ego-head.

We finally made it thru the winter but the dog was still a coming event for the spring and summer just ahead. I conceived a plan that I felt might help correct the situation. I purchased a four foot by eight-foot sheet of plywood and painted both sides white. I lettered both sides with the following message in black six-inch high characters. I placed the sign near the street next the north property line in full view of his front picture window as well as street traffic from either direction.

DOG DUMPING GROUNDS

CLOSED

ENTIRE MONTH OF JUNE

TO ALLOW TIME TO

PREPARE FOR THE

SUMMER

This sign worked like a charm and only needed the first two weeks of June to remedy a stinky situation.

DC Mooning Girl

Owning a pick-up camper manufacturing business (Hobo Mfg.) gave me an opportunity to build a very special camper for our own use. The camper I built was equipped with all the latest appliances, toilet and a large picture window in the sleeping area above the cab.

Betty and I decided to make a trip to Washington D C with the camper and our five kids plus a borrowed neighbor kid. We made it to Pennsylvania Avenue in front of the White House in heavy stop and go traffic. Betty and I were in the cab and all six kids were in the bed over the cab supposedly taking in the sights of our nation's capital through the large window.

We noticed several pedestrians looking up at our camper window laughing and pointing occasionally as if counting heads. The traffic stoppage was not an inconvenience since it gave us an opportunity to look around while stopped. It was not until some-time later that we found out what was so hilarious to the people in the street. One of our older sons was pulling our (Karen about 2 yrs. old) youngest daughter's pants down and mooning the general public in D C.

Camper Caper

A good friend of mine called me and invited me and my two oldest boys to go ice fishing on Lake St. Clair (the baby great lake). Owning a nice pick-up camper and truck, I volunteered to use it for the fishing trip since he also had a son that would go along and that way we could have plenty of room for everyone plus take alone refreshments and food for the day. My friend brought a gallon of hard cider that he and I could sip to combat the cold out on the ice. We started out early Saturday morning and my oldest son had invited a neighborhood buddy along which made a total of four boys in their early teens to ride in the camper while my friend and I enjoyed the peace and quiet of the truck cab for the hour long trip to the lake.

All went well and according to plan. We cut ice holes several places for the boys and ourselves, but the fish surely must have seen what our plans were. They all seemed to go somewhere else so we retired back to the camper shortly after noon, warmed our frozen toes ate some sandwiches. The boys had had enough and strongly suggested that we return home since they could spend the rest of the day at some other activity without adults checking out their every move.

My friend and I had hardly sipped the hard cider while out on the ice, so we put it in the refrigerator for the hour long trip back home. During the ride home our second oldest son decided to taste the hard cider even though he had been denied earlier. Of course one taste was not enough, consequently when we arrived home he was in no condition to spend the rest of the day with the other boys as originally planned. He was not only very sick but inebriated and in considerable trouble along with me and Mom.

Speed Demon Mom

Our family of five children at the time of this story consisted of three boys about sixteen, thirteen and eleven with two sisters that seldom created situations of concern.

However, it's the Mom's love for speed that reminds me to recall the following.

The youngest boy "Terry" made friends with another boy his age a couple of streets away who had a home-made go-cart. Of course, pressure was brought to bear on me to help him build a go-cart. Our subdivision consisted of about five streets of mostly young families and our home was on the outer side with an open field behind. The streets of low-profile hills afforded good coasting downhill activity.

A go-cart project was completed consisting of an eight foot long 2 x 8 fuselage with a pair of bicycle wheels mounted to cross seating boards. The front wheels of smaller diameter were attached with a centered pivot bolt at the and a steering wheel column. This wood body "motor-less" model soon created advancement activity. Up-hill navigation limited the activities enjoyment somewhat.

Road-worthiness testing was spread over the next few weeks with design modifications here and there (motorization) eventually persisted. Listening to the evening meal discussions, I determined faster and faster road tests were coming, and soon the motorized model shown here evolved. I established some testing track geography concerning cross street avoidance. There seemed to be a certain favorite cross street intersection hill or even our driveway.

Returning home one afternoon after a day of work I approached the favorite cross street intersection to find, not only my youngest son, but <u>driving a go-cart was his mother</u>. I was flabbergasted and reiterated all the precautionary measures Mom had directed, however she also enjoyed the speeding "motorized" action too

Improved model (not the Mom she was perfect), see what I mean?

Professional Archer

Our oldest son and his best neighbor friend were obsessed with developing their skill at target shooting with bow and arrow. They had prepared a shooting range in the wooded back yard and were spending hour upon hour shooting arrows at a bull's eye target. Their range consisted of two or three markers for shooting distances. Upon returning home from work one day, with a fair amount of paperwork for review in hand, I discovered the two boys practicing archery skills. At the insistence of my son that I watch as they launched a few arrows at the target with varying degrees' accuracy none of which came close to the bull's eye, I chided them with gentle criticism.

Of course, this brought on a challenge from them. I claimed that they were much too close to the target and that I could probably out shoot them at twice the distance they had been using. At their insistence an immediate demonstration of my skill was required. Still dressed in my business suit and a full bundle of business papers made little sympathy from them as to whether I should be excused from showing my skill immediately if not sooner. Being pressured to either "put up or shut up" I agreed to shoot one arrow from a distance twice that of what they had been using. They snickered as I carefully placed my important papers on the lawn and borrowed one arrow and a bow. Having also had considerable archery experience behind me as a teen age boy, I knew that embarrassment was only a few minutes away. Low and behold my carefully launched arrow hit the center of the bull's eye, as the two amazed boys claimed luck over skill and insisted a repeat performance was in order to validate my skill. Of course I excused myself from further demonstration since I had important paperwork to review and I was not dressed for the activity.

Gary's Determination

The first day of senior year High School for Gary prompted him to go to school dressed up since it was a special day for making good impressions. He decided to go to first day wearing a neck-tie. Since this was not necessarily the usual dress code he was chided by his best neighborhood friend for wearing a necktie to school. Gary informed his friend that he was sure this was simply a sign of maturity and more young men should dress-up occasionally. This only added to the tease and intensity of disagreement, so Gary proposed a $5.00 bet that he could wear a necktie every school day in his senior year. His good friend foolishly accepted the bet challenge. Gary's determination served him well and he won the bet but I really don't know if he collected.

Work Attitude

Our desire to teach responsible work and job attitudes for our young family of three oldest boys and two girls caused us to create what we considered a foolproof set of ground-rules. The following set of incidents is an example of how the best of intentions do not always produce anticipated results. When the boys began to enter their teen years, the desire to possess worldly goods developed just like some of their middle class friends.   We had never given an allowance of money to our children unless it was earned in some form or fashion consisting mostly of household duty assignments. Now I don't want to imply that our children were denied necessities or even acceptable social experiences, but the house rule was "if you want something, you need to earn its cost".

This rule almost worked well if you refused to consider that it might be easier just to do the chore yourself, or accept the inefficiency and ignore the management aspects. An appropriate extra money allowance was usually decided when teen age was achieved, which worked pretty well until such time as the household chore allowance money was inadequate for the necessary costs of teen survival. Eventually outside employment was more attractive and far more monetarily rewarding, so again family rules were reviewed and up-graded as follows.

If you take a job outside our home,
you can't quit unless you have a better
one.

Our oldest son Gary found a job delivering newspapers which was a seven day a week task that entailed early morning deliveries mostly in our middle class neighborhood, however it was not entirely effortless since certain time or weather conditions required mom to chauffer the route by automobile. This job lasted for quite some-time until Gary reached an employment age allowing him to become an ice-cream clerk paying more money.

Our second oldest son Daniel decided that he would like to take Gary's old job as a newspaper deliverer because he wanted a new bicycle, especially since his old one was not as good as his friends were riding. Again Mom was saddled with un-wanted chauffer duties, due to weather or time conditions enhanced by additional devised excuses for assistance. Several informal requests were made to Mom to let the newspaper route go which she ignored and attempted to remind him of the monetary gains he enjoyed.   One evening (in June 1965) as we all sat down to the dinner table, I sensed an air of tension among the remainder of the family and soon discovered the reason. All the children were strangely quiet and there had been some heavily discussed situation beforehand. Betty informed me that I needed to read a note lying under my dinner plate. Upon opening the note, inscrolled on school notepaper, was the following message.

DO NOT READ ALOUD

Dear ol Dad,

I would like to Quit my paper route before you answer read the rest of this note. I think I should be able to quit because a lot of guys want my route and I have not fooled around on it like Gary does and I don't want a mini bike and any way I have a three speed bike and I have enough money for to suit me and I can get little jobs for extra money and any way let me quit.

DANNY MILLER

Silence permeated the air while I interrogated the situation, discovering no replacement job. Although I was certain Betty wanted relief from the chauffeuring, we stood our ground, fortunately Danny found a different job with a landscape nursery, however the following results played out showing, "best of intentions do not always produce anticipated results".

Having witnessed his older brother's entrapment, our third son Terry chose not to obtain outside employment until he was nearly seventeen, apparently teen sacrifice of worldly possessions was not all that bad, since home jobs were mostly by choice.

Fooling the Airlines

Back in the 1970s I was required to travel many times to various Industrial Hygiene Seminars representing our company as designers and producers of compressed air purification equipment for furnishing grade "D" breathing air to workers in hazardous work areas. In addition to the purification equipment for "show and tell" being shipped via commercial truck, we also had two large metal trunk-type <u>carry-on</u> display containers. These trunks were as large as overseas luggage trunks and were always a handling problem even though we could strap them together and depend on <u>baggage</u> handlers to assist to the plane. (Incidentally, this would never work in today's travel accommodations) We never trusted the commercial shippers since these trunks contained the necessary display artwork, customer interest applications and much other product specific information.

It was always Friday afternoon to travel back home along with every other business traveler so the home trip was always a little more tedious. Some-times you might have to put up with as much as a 15-minute delayed departure and this was always an aggravation in addition to handling the two hellish big trunks on board.

I devised a unique plan to avoid having to handle the display trunks when I arrived back at my home airport by checking these trunks as baggage. When baggage was conveyed into the home airport, I would simply pick up only my personal luggage, and approach the lost baggage desk to report the trunks missing. As a result, the airline would deliver the missing trunks direct to our office the next Monday

Fooling the Competition

I worked as General Manager several years for a company producing industrial hygiene equipment. We had a competitor exhibitor in air purification equipment manufacturing business and they almost always displayed in the same Industrial Hygiene Seminars that we did. A neat technique had been devised for gathering names and addresses of potential customers. An embossed plastic identity card issued to attendee's containing their information could be rolled over a courtesy card device making a duplicate under with a carbon paper sandwiched between. This process was very similar to the original charge card process before graduating into electronic transmissions. We exhibitors would keep the copy for back home office follow up and the potential customer would keep the card displaying our exhibitor's name. The carbon was dispatched into the trash basket under a display table. We would always wait around after closing time until the competition had left the area. We would then empty their trash into our trash thereby gathering carbon copies of all their contacts of the day. We always joked about running a trash collection business.

Age Discovery

Two incidents come to mind when I think about discovering your true age. The first is a story related to me by a friend in St. Charles when we were teenagers. A neighborhood movie theatre was operated by Mr. and Mrs. Lessing. They were a childless couple and enjoyed the kids in the area and were considerably tolerant to the antics that took place from time to time at The Ritz. The fare for a movie was ten cents for children under 16 and twenty-five cents for adults. My friend was over 17 years old but had never bought an adult ticket because he would always approach Mrs. Lessing in the ticket booth crouching down and placing a dime on the counter. His age discovery came one time when he presented a quarter for his ticket and received a smile, a thank you and an adult ticket.

Many years later while working as Plant Manager for a small manufacturing company in Ferndale, MI I was rudely made aware of my early 50s age. Sometimes I would leave the plant and have lunch at a nearby restaurant that served good food. One day my secretary (about 20 years old) had asked me if I was going out for lunch and if I had ever eaten at the nice restaurant down the street. I answered in the affirmative and she asked if I cared to take her along. Flattered by this request, I said sure and I will even buy. On the way down the street, I decided to drive thru the carwash to get the car cleaned up. I gave the attendant a ten-dollar bill and he handed me change which I handed to my secretary to hold until I could put it in my pocket. When we got to the restaurant she handed me the change consisting of eight dollars. I immediately commented that the guy had made a mistake of two dollars and my secretary smilingly informed me "*No they only charge $2.00 for senior citizens*".

Getting My Money

The year of 1968, a friend of mine sold his "kellering" tool machine shop on Mound road to some "wanna-be" guys who thought they were going to "take" the auto industry big time. My friend Roy told me that they had big-talked G M Oldsmobile into an after-market job, furnishing replacement valve rocker arms for the "62" engine. He indicated they had no idea as far as he could tell what they were thinking, taking on a production job like that when all the machines in the shop were metal cutting equipment for tooling. He suggested that I should "help them" out. So I looked over the prints and promptly reminded them that they had no grinding equipment to produce the close tolerance compound curve on the valve end of the forged rocker arm.

After they had unsuccessfully attempted to get outside bids (all were more than the job was worth) I told them that I could grind these for $.25 cents each plus the cost of tooling for the job. The tooling consisted of reworking an old horizontal mill by attaching a tooling plate on the over arm to hold parts and mounting a grinding machine spindle on the saddle after removing the old table. The tooling plate was grooved and an eccentric drive bearing created a swinging motion, which represented one of the radii while the other radius was diamond dressed into the face of the grinding wheel. All this was simple and produced five finished parts in approximately 60 seconds cycle time.

I was obviously pleased with the prospect of making about $75.00 an hour when labor was going for about $5.50 at that time. I had set up this machine in my garage at home in Rochester. I installed blinds on the windows to keep neighbors out of my business, however since each time the tooling plate made a swing over the parts being ground, sparks would fly which appeared odd at night. I intercepted a few phone calls of concern that something was sparking in my garage.

Obviously I had not indicated to my shop friends where my machine was located and every-thing was going fine. I was paying my son $10.00 an hour and everyone was happy until GM decided that they needed to certify the manufacturing processes. Although my machine produced acceptable parts, the process had to be moved into the (wanna-be boys) city shop on Mound road.

I knew immediately that big problems would arrive as soon as the "wanna-be's" found out that I could make $75.00 an hour when they were having a hard time getting $45.00 hour for their entire shop rate. Sure enough they began to slow pay me and soon they owed me $4,345.00. Each time I called for money I would get another promise but no money.

I decided to bring pressure the way I had been taught to collect from slow payers, so I went into their shop one night about 10:00 PM and told the night foreman I needed to remove my grinding spindle for rework. I stripped my machine of every- thing that I could but before leaving I loaded a finished injection mold (ready for shipment to Ford) on my truck.

Next morning about 8:00 I called Bill (wanna-be) but before I could say anything, he said *"We got some money coming this week and we can probably pay you"*. I very nicely said *"Bill, I just called to ask if you guys are missing anything this morning"*. The silence was deafening for a full minute and then unprintable words came at me with the threat *"you don't know who you are fooling with"*. I calmly replied *"Yes Bill, I know very well that I am dealing with people who don't pay their bills, but I think I may know where the Ford mold can be found if you can find my $4,345.00"*. The phone went dead.

About 9:00 AM I received a call from a Warren City police detective who decided that this was a civil case and not a criminal action since I had not forcibly obtained the mold.

Five minutes later Bill (wanna-be) called and said *"I have your @#%^&* money as soon as you get here with that mold"*. I replied *"Bill I want cash or a certified check and it is to be delivered to Oakland Welding shop in Pontiac at 11:00"*. *At 11:00,* Bills brother Buddy (wanna-be #2) arrived at Oakland welding wearing his $500.00 suit and driving a big Cadillac.

He told me to back my truck into the hi-bay and his truck would back in for the mold transfer using the overhead crane. I smiled and said--

"No, your truck backs into the hi-bay and then I will back in, but first nothing happens until I get the money".

He smiled and said *"It's here in my inside suit pocket, look"*.

Aside the check was a shoulder holster holding a big revolver handgun. This bothered me but I calculated that he wouldn't dare use that pistol with a shop full of witnesses. As I reached for the check he closed his suit and informed me that when the mold was on his truck, I would get the check.

I then told him that I would have the mold lifted and held one inch above his truck bed and that is when the check was to be handed over. He hesitated but after surveying the number of people who were watching the show he agreed. We placed our trucks as agreed.

As soon as he handed me the check I instructed the crane operator to place the mold, as I handed the certified check over to my friend the owner of Oakland Welding for safe keeping. I then drove my truck out of the way and Buddy's truck driver left the premises with the mold.

Bill's (wanna-be #2) brother Buddy sat in his Cadillac on the street for a while. I suspect he was thinking

"Maybe I could retrieve the check". However, I enjoyed a couple cups of coffee in the office with my welding shop friends which included a policeman friend of theirs that usually stopped by for a cup in the morning. Buddy (wanna be #2) finally drove away and the policeman friend escorted me out of town.

About a year or so later my friend, Roy who had sold his machine shop to Bill and brothers foreclosed on the shop. He told me that the story about how I had gotten my money was all over town, and my method was the same as used by the Mafia in some cases. The Buzzo brothers should have been familiar with it.

Another one…

This money collecting tactic had been taught to me by my rough and tumble mentor boss and shop owner who had moved me and family to Michigan. We were doing a small amount of work from time to time for the giant Ford Motor Company experimental department. While they were at least a thousand times bigger than us they were a little disrespectful of our unique machining ability. We had only one competitor in the country and did not consider ourselves as a usual parts supplier whom they typically abused. They had placed an occasional order for experimental components from time to time, but had developed a habit of not paying our invoices for ninety days or more. We had just completed a special deep hole drilling operation for them being developed for an experimental transmission design.

My mentor boss instructed me to call them too send their truck and pick up their completed parts which would not be loaded unless the driver had a check for the dollar amount of the invoice in my hand. The amazed buyer could not believe his ears when I gave him this message and immediately transferred me to the manager of purchasing.

His angry question to me was "Do you know who you are dealing with?" and I simply reported that we were dealing with a company who didn't pay their bills on time. "Ford Motor Company will **never** place another order with you, do you understand?" I simply answered "O K".

And another one...

A few years later I had formed my company Hammermaster with the prospect of earning my living doing building contracting and thoughts of buying and selling remodeled homes. My contacts with a large lumber company introduced me to a manufacturing company who had set up a shop producing "do-it-yourself" kits for small back yard utility sheds. The kit contained all the precut components of studs, roof trusses, roof skin and walls in a convenient cardboard boxed container.

They were looking for a contractor to assemble these at various lumber yards as displays. The shed was designed for the typical home owner to assemble with nails furnished and they had agreed to pay me $100.00 per display shed at their lumber yard customer locations. I was also allowed to solicit home buyers who cared not to do their own assembly. I assembled the first shed using air tools and began developing some "one man" tools since the manager of the manufacturing company assumed I would need a helper.

With tools and air hammers, I was able to construct a shed in a little over an hour. I had made an agreement to take a consignment of four packaged sheds on my car hauler trailer. Everything was moving along nicely and I was making fair money all by myself until the owner of the shop found out I didn't need a helper so he wanted me to reduce my invoices proportionately. He began to slow pay me and it soon became necessary to hold four sheds at my house, **so he paid up just as I had been taught he would do.**

Greedy Lawyer (Hobo sale)

In 1966 Bill Beggs and I had started on a part time basis a pick-up camper manufacturing company which we named HOBO Mfg. Co. Bill's full time job as CEO of Pontiac Bushing Co. required him to move to a more favorable labor market area in Indiana, so we agreed for me to buy (transfer) the business. This was done very simply by compiling a dollar value list of inventory items which I bought (**transferred interests**) over a cup of coffee and some genuine USA cash dollars from my pocket to his pocket.

I quit my full time job as Executive Vice President of 20th Century Machine Company to expand the business since a current rage at that time was pick-up campers and motor homes for travel. The market was hot and I had discussed the possibility of a business loan with my banker which he assured me would be available when I was ready to expand into a volume operation. I had established a couple of dealers in the local area and began building production fixtures and plans while building some prototype campers. Several months had gone by before I could prepare adequately for the bank loan. Unfortunately, the economic atmosphere had taken a downward turn by the time I was ready and the banker simply informed me that lending money was no longer available.

In the mean-time Ford Motor Company had jumped into the pick-up camper manufacturing business with a camper known as the "Goldline". I reasoned that since their camper was basically two fiberglass halves designed for volume production and they possessed established dealerships everywhere, I was headed for big trouble. I continued to build campers basically one at a time for the next year or so and managed to get the attention of GMC Truck Company, however unknown to me was GMC's entry into the market with a line of motor homes.

I had sold a shell camper to a neighbor Jack McGregor with the agreement that he could custom finish on my company lot in the evenings. We became good friends over the next few weeks and since I was financially stressed by this time he proposed to buy my company and operate it as an after work hour's activity. We agreed upon a price from my inventory list much the same way that I had previously done, however someone informed him that he should get a lawyer to look over the deal. I told him that I didn't want the expense of a lawyer so he said why don't we share the cost and I said "OK find a cheap one".

We met at the lawyer's office near Jacks work and he mumbled some legalese about a "*bulk **transfer** act*", but that he couldn't represent both of us. When we assured him that since neither of us was interested in cheating, we could dispense with legal representation. He quickly said that maybe he could review the paperwork after all for payment up front. Jack said, "OK I'll pay you" and paid him cash during his lunch break from his job the next day. That same afternoon the lawyer called me at Hobo Mfg. and asked me to bring cash to his office for his work. When Jack and I met the next day we realized that the "bulk **transfer**" jargon was actually about our money transferring from **us to him**. We decided that mud-slinging just gets you dirty especially if your target is a dirty lawyer. Both of us remained clean and brighter, *Aunt Hattie, I forgot all about you again.*

Jack and I had agreed that I could retain the drawings I had made of the Hobo camper structure. We had become good friends and I jokingly told him the drawings represented "intellectual property" and he mentioned several times he knew where to obtain superior intellect.

About six months went by and one day I came upon my drawings and suddenly realized I should make a mail order information "do-it-yourself" kit for the many people out there that could use drawings, bill of material and guidance to build their own pick-up camper. I placed a couple of small ads in the back pages of sports magazines and over the next year or so enjoyed going to the post office and picking up checks from all over, even from a few other countries.

Business start-ups are difficult and I just remembered another incident concerning the Hobo camper ownership. While developing the camper I made an acquaintance with a fellow who worked for GMC as a Product Advertising Manager. He was interested in my development of the Hobo pick-up camper and offered to display a prototype at the outdoor GMC Michigan state fair in 1967. I was elated at the opportunity to be exposed at such a prestigious location but he made me aware that he would not be able to furnish a truck, but his department was allocated a truck for display and agreed to sell it to me after the fair at cost.

This represented a financial kick in the pants but we shook hands on the agreement. He then asked me to have appropriate hand bills for the general public at the fair-grounds. I contacted another person whom I had used in the past who had promoted for a previous employer. He prepared all the hand-bill artwork in color and I was stuck with a minimum order of one thousand at $.10 cents each. The fair was a six-day task at which I attended, handing out literature. First evening after closing time as I was leaving the fair grounds, I was aghast to see my hand-outs lying all up and down the fairway. For the remainder of the show you better bet I was careful to squeeze genuine interest out before you could get an expensive $.10 cent color brochure out of me.

I later found out GMC management had decided to get into the recreational vehicular business for their small trucks as well as developing a motor home product line. I am pretty sure I had been used for new product intelligence since the truck I had to buy was the very first camper special they had built since the chrome insignias "*camper special*" on each side were installed at the fairgrounds.

Production campers awaiting dealer delivery & MI State Fair display.

Bad Check Collector

I need to digress from the above story a bit, so this is about a character I met.

This situation developed as I was busy building "Hobo" truck campers. My manufacturing company was located in an old farm barn on Auburn road, just east of Pontiac. A neighborhood tavern was just up the street and they had a short order cooking area at one end of the bar where I could get a sandwich for lunch. Jack McGregor and I had eaten there several times and one day one of the bar stool regulars came over to our booth and offered to buy us a beer. We politely refused and he proceeded to inquire as to our activities since he had noticed us there several times before.

We explained that I was developing a product line of pickup campers and intended to market them soon. In the meantime, I was selling prototypes as the tooling for production was being developed.

He immediately began to disclose his back ground and experiences. First off, he was a reformed alcoholic, but enjoyed buying drinks for friends occasionally (*this was why he was in that tavern quite often*), and he operated a very successful telephone promotion business a few blocks down the street. Jack and I simply listened politely (*he was at least 30 years older than us*) and soon excused ourselves to return to the shop, after he had asked of the location with a promise of a visit sometime.

He wore eyeglasses' as thick as pop bottle bottoms and had a very aggressive, but friendly approach and claimed that he had some talents that could be very useful to a guy just getting started in business. Back at the shop Jack and I had several comments about the old bar-fly that didn't drink claiming connections that could be very helpful. We dismissed most everything except his existence and decided that we would find another lunch place if needed. Within the next week our bar acquaintance showed up at the shop door and politely asked if he could visit for a few minutes. I was overwhelmed at his friendliness and persistence, but decided to allow him a short tour around the shop (*besides he might know somebody that needed a pick-up camper*). It took probably all of 15 minutes to show him the tooling and plans for production I had in mind when he said *"let's sit in the office and let me think how I might help you"*.

I was becoming very suspicious of his interest in my well-being, but decided to invest a couple more minutes before ejecting him from my life. We sat down and before I could start conversation, he peered at the wall behind my desk through his thick glasses. I had tacked a "bad check" given to me by a customer there. He asked about it and I explained that I had attempted to collect from the guy several times to no avail. With a very positive attitude, he asked *"You want your money? Give me that check and I will get the bastard to bring your money to your house tonight. You want him roughed up or just the money?"* I replied that the money was all I needed, while thinking to myself *(This old guy is a real nut, but give him the worthless paper to get rid of him).*

At about 8:00 that evening after supper, there was a knock on my front door. Opening the door I found the deadbeat check writer begging me to take the cash he was holding and apologizing for any trouble he may have caused.

Next day my newfound mentor called to confirm that I had received my money and that he had not even needed to have the guy roughed up. I inquired as to how he had been able to perform the collection that I had been trying for several weeks. He simply admitted that he had many friends to help in situations like that and among them was Mr. Hoffa and that nobody could hide from the thousands of eyes of the teamsters.

My friend became a lunch companion many times after that and I was never able to dispute his claims. Some of which I will outline so you can enjoy a bit of the character I was privileged to meet.

The lunch tavern had a raised area at one end with a baby grand piano for music in the evenings I suppose. One-day Jack, my bad check collector and I were lunching in a booth as some person was hammering away on the piano. Being somewhat tone deaf, the efforts were of no particular concern to me, but our friend winced almost as in pain several times. The piano player departed to the men's room and immediately my friend excused himself and approached the raised platform, but not having good eyesight stumbled in the darkened room while approaching the raised area. He regained his footing and sat down at the piano as Jack and I heard the guy in the next booth mutter *"dammed drunks and their piano playing"*. Soon the room was filled with the most accomplished classical music that barroom had ever heard.

Although my new friend was alcoholic he mentored alcoholics in jail several weekends a month since he possessed personal knowledge and also possessed a PHD in Psychology. There seemed to be no end to the people he knew and the things he had done, and neither Jack nor I could find any untruths in his stories.

I was somewhat dubious of his claim of operating a successful fundraising *(commonly called a boiler-room)* business from his home, so upon his invitation I visited there to verify. Upon entering we were greeted by his wife who was likely younger than myself, beautiful and gracious. In a large back room, was probably twelve or fifteen seated guys lined up in a row partitioned from each other, with telephone lines coming down from the ceiling into each work space. Each guy was intent in telephone conversation and paper records. The telephone cable entering the room was likely four inches or more in diameter. My friend claimed he collected a percentage of pledges obtained for charities, churches, political or any other client they could help.

My friend claimed that it was he who conceived the Ford Motor company logo of the light bulb claiming a "better idea". He said he had sold it to them for a reasonable sum of money?

He also claimed that he was traveling by train one time with the Spike Jones band when they were stuck in a snowstorm for a day. Together they created the hit tune for

Spike Jones "I got a gal in Kalamazoo". Spike Jones
enjoyed success by inserting weird noises and inappropriate
sounds into otherwise popular orchestral presentations.

One day my friend came to the shop very excited and
asked

"Hey Miller, you got any money?"

I just looked at him and replied

"Do I look like it?"

Whereas he pushed a little harder and said

"Just a couple a thousand will make you a million"

"What do we have to do, rob banks?"

*"No, me and some other Jews are going to build a
stadium in Pontiac and take   the Tigers, Red Wings &
Pistons away from Detroit."*

I scoffed and dismissed the opportunity due to
financial embarrassment. Sure enough the Silver Dome
arena was built within a couple of years under budget and on
time.

My Dad always said *"Them that has - gits"* and
"Them that hasn't - frets" but any way I still couldn't
believe my friend who knew about the Silver Dome arena
before it happened.

Girls Clean Your Room—Prelude

Living in that middle to upper class neighborhood
sort of established some habitat standards set by Mom.
These were not entirely difficult or unfair standards,
however continuous maintenance and attention was required
for the entire household. The penalty for failure to conform
could range all the way from a verbal request to intensive
persuasion by Mom, but if that encouragement failed to
produce acceptable results in a timely fashion the infraction

could be referred to the highest enforcer in the form of an exasperated plea.

Among Moms standards of occupancy was (*Keep your belongings picked up and put in an acceptable place*). This was necessary as far as Mom was concerned to establish respectability of our home in the neighborhood, in case we had guests that could destroy a reputation with a "flap of a lip" so to speak.

Now, in all fairness I must admit that my ability to meet this standard did not always conform too Mom's level of acceptability especially in the garage/workshop area. But, on the other hand nobody of importance "lip flapper type" was ever invited to that area anyway. I attempted to remove the big things for safety's sake but sometimes the smaller items were left where used last.

With the passage of time, we have all been educated as to personality characteristics that are inherent due to Genes, Environment and Moms persistence. I suppose this could be disastrous if I were criminal, but I'm not (just a little sloppy) sometimes. However, the story here is about my two daughters and some inherited characteristics.

Girls Clean Your Room

In about the year of 1969 our family had grown to the point of full bedroom capacity. The two girls were sharing a bedroom and there was nearly a continual request (*pick up your room)* which more times than not, accusations ensued about who made the mess. This would invariable create a decision by Mom

"*I don't care who did it, either clean it up or suffer the consequences.*"

One evening upon returning home after a nerve wracking day at my job, Mom greeted me with one more problem of which I was in no mood to deal with.

"I have been after the girls to pick up their room for the last two hours, all they will do is ignore me because they have neighbor kids in the yard, so you can handle it."

Frustration and lack of diplomacy sometimes create "never forgotten" results along with the achievement of success. While the girls were busy entertaining friends outside I decided to add a little emphasis to the slightly unkempt room. I proceeded to turn their beds upside down in the middle of the floor, remove all clothing from the two closets and pile them on the bed mixed together of course. I removed every childhood toy, trinket or doll from the wrap-around shelf board (that I had built for them) and piled them on the bed as well as emptying all dresser drawers into the pile. It was a beautiful disaster site to behold as my frustrations were pleasingly appeased.

The girls were instructed to come:

NOW, CLEAN YOUR ROOM

Many years have passed, but evidence seems to point out which one was the biggest mess maker and perhaps the many times ignored plea of innocence was unjust. But that's life and perhaps my bummer genes should take full responsibility. They have both turned out as responsible, perfect adults so maybe abuse builds character?

Tragedy Missed

Our home was tri level design consisting of the main living area being a ground level concrete floor including a two car garage just off a family room. Some kids up the street had a plastic swimming pool in the back yard and our kids had been invited to play in it a couple of times. It seems that some of the kids in the pool were not being monitored properly by adults and Betty rescinded permission to visit that pool. This brought on an immediate vocal rebellion including claims that we were not being fair as far as allowing swimming pool play. The rebellion eventually worked and a plastic pool was bought to reduce the complaints of childhood needs.

Our property was pie shaped and the house was built into a hillside having a small street frontage and a large rear area covered with trees and a tiny creek at the back. I certainly did not want the plastic pool in the front yard and there was no level place anywhere else to place the pool. I decided that a reasonable alternative was to put the pool in the two-car garage even though it filled the entire floor area with just enough room to pass by it into the house. (*Don't even think about it-I DIDN'T*) I reasoned that this was also a good solution since the kids would be essentially protected from sunburn while the garage door was kept open so it nearly felt like an outside atmosphere.

All went well for the first couple of weeks, however one evening upon returning home from work I noticed the ceiling gypsum board was wet from kids belly flopping into the water. At the dinner table I began to outline the proper use of the swimming pool in the garage and the biggest rule was that no more belly flopping since the water damage to the ceiling was a serious tragedy that must be eliminated. The second rule to be adhered too was no more tracking into the house with wet feet and clothes. I thought the reasons and rules had been understood and the water control situation was settled, however a few days later the kids had invited some friends over to play in their indoor pool. When I came home that evening I was aghast at the water deposited on the ceiling again and upon closer inspection the gypsum ceiling was beginning to separate from the overhead joists.

The following day the pool was removed from its indoor garage home. The missed tragedy, discovered later was the amount of water that could very well been dispatched directly into the family and living room area of our house if a side wall rupture had occurred.

Incidentally another missed tragedy with that home, was part of the foundation had been placed on fill soil. Betty called me at work one day and informed me the floor in the family room had a crack in the tiles running diagonally across the room. When I came home later that day the crack had begun to cross all the way from two outside walls and I knew that a movement going downhill including the fireplace was taking place. I called the builder and he came over and nonchalantly said he could have his guys take up the tile and patch the crack in the floor. I was enraged by this and informed him that I wanted a certified stress engineer to direct an underpinning fix.

He refused this approach so I contacted a local lawyer the next day to begin forcing him to correct his work. Unfortunately, the lawyer I contacted after two unsuccessful meetings, I began to sense a certain lack of interest in the faulty construction problem. I then asked around and found out the lawyer was a distant relative to the builder. I immediately obtained a new lawyer from another city and soon the builders attitude changed and accepted the recommendations of a professional stress engineer for the placement of several yards of underpinning on virgin soil to stop further movement downhill of the southwest corner of my house. The tragedy I missed was pointed out to me a year or so later when my neighbors two story house by the same builder lost its west wall due to the foundation being placed on fill soil and a major repair had to be made.

One-And-A-Half Bathing Suits

1966 Having moved to Michigan a few years earlier, I was constantly urged to go up north and discover the Au Sable River. I decided to take my two oldest sons and explore for a weekend. We loaded fishing gear and embarked on the trip very early in the morning. When arriving in the town of Grayling where the river is located, we discovered a canoe rental business. They were located right on the river and would pick you up downstream at certain designated places agreed upon and portage the canoe back to Grayling. We made an agreement and started floating downstream enjoying the countryside and the fast running clear water stream.

The river was usually about 30 feet wide in most places and it appeared to be a really good place to fish. At about 10:00 in the morning we came upon a small island in the middle of the stream about 50 feet long and about 20 feet wide with small trees and bushes growing on it. I beached the canoe on the gravel at the upstream end of the island and told the boys we would do some fishing from the bank of this island. The boys stationed themselves at the canoe end of the island since that was near the packages of cookies their mother had packed for them.

I took my fishing rod and some lures to the downstream end of the island with a plan to cast with the current. The stream divided by the island, essentially making two streams about 10 or 15 feet wide on each side, however one side was partially blocked with a fallen fir tree from the shore near my end of the island.

Near the town of Grayling was a military training camp that was used for weekend activities and many times the wives of the servicemen would accompany them to the town. The canoe rental company enjoyed the business created by influx of short term trips of some of these ladies and today was no exception since two or three canoes with kids and adults had passed by me on the navigable side of my island.

Shortly after I began to fish off my little gravel station two lady canoeists selected the wrong fork of the stream at the upstream end and were being rushed directly into the overhanging tree limbs. Upon discovering the mistake, the lady in the front of the canoe began commanding her backseat driver to reverse. The driver kept explaining that she couldn't and was desperately back paddling to no avail.

In the meantime, the lady in the front wearing a two-piece bathing suit had become entangled in the grasp of the fir tree limbs. The force of the swift water had caused her to slowly sink down backwards in the seat as one of the limbs had grasped her bathing suit top. She was unable to untangle her arms down from their overhead position and was screaming desperately at her partner to stop while she was being disrobed. I was only a few feet away and could not avoid the entire procedure, had I chose.

The driver lady was smarter and nimbly ducked forward into the canoe bottom as it passed under the grasping tree. The bathing suit top remained on the tree limb and as the half clothed lady went by me she red-faced exclaimed to me

"Nothing like this ever happened to me before."
I smilingly replied
"Me either."

224

The last I saw of them, they were desperately trying to decide whether to stop and return to the site or not. I have always wondered what took place after they went out of site downstream. I was truly tempted to retrieve the bathing suit top, but thought better not to get involved.

Best Costume

We were in our late forty's and a good friend had invited Betty & me to attend a Halloween costume party at his club. I had asked him several times how the party was going to be run such as, *"was there dancing and was there prizes for the best costume?"* He bragged that he was well connected in the club and when it came to costuming prizes he would likely beat me. Seems that he knew all the judges and the judging would be on the dance floor just before the dance music started, his attitude piqued me somewhat.

When it comes to fun, it's part of my heritage to take no prisoners when having fun as a "challenge".

The big night came and the four of us rode together in the same car. I had carefully made costume plans, and had packed it all into a paper grocery bag so as not to expose the strategy to my challenger. Meantime he had gone to a considerable amount of work to dress as a pirate complete with an eye patch, unwieldy sword, hot leather pants, and as many other cumbersome and uncomfortable dressings as you can think of.

He looked at my little bag and sneered that he was assured of a prize if that's all I could think of, as a costume.

The party was a bit slow to start because food was presented first, then the dance floor was cleared for the parade of costumers to "show and tell". I enjoyed immensely his efforts to eat with his eye patch in place and his sword sticking in the way of every one including him.

After food I immediately went into the men's room with my bagged costume which consisted of an ankle length red & white striped flannel nightgown complete with a long tasseled matching nightcap, a candle holder with candle, and a small pillow. I left my shoes and socks in the bag, sleepily strolled barefoot onto the dance floor center with a lighted candle, yawing, ignoring the costumed parade as they circled the floor. I very ceremoniously puffed out the candle, placed my pillow on the floor, yawned as long as I dared, placed my candle, laid my head on the pillow and went immediately to sleep. My performance was superb and uninterrupted as guests giggled and enjoyed.

The master of ceremony helped me out with some comments such as-

"Must be a boring party. Hope none of the lady's join him."

The costume parade lasted for a considerable time while the judges were busy making notes, but I remained fast asleep in the middle of the dance floor. The MC began to announce winners and prizes were given out, my friend didn't make it, and I remained in my sleep mode.

The costumers all went back to their respective tables, but I remained asleep as the dance music began. Finally, the MC stopped the orchestra and announced that if someone would volunteer to take a consolation prize out to the sleeping guy, maybe he would clear the floor. My friend brought me a six pack and begrudgingly admitted defeat as he escorted me from the center of the floor.

How Not-To Treat Antique Nuts

We were being visited by our good friends (Corky & Clarice) from out of town. A couple of days after the initial visit was over the girls decided to attend an auction that was advertised as an estate sale. The sale was outside a large farmhouse and the items offered were strewn everywhere. We drove our station wagon and had parked in the driveway early in the day close to the many items that were to be sold. It was a beautiful sunshine day and the girls had decided that they were going to bid on the many antique picture frames lined up among all the other household furnishings.   Corky and I sat dutifully in the wagon and told lies to each other, played gin and dozed off for most of the afternoon.

Occasionally we would make a trip through the bidders as the sing-song auctioneer worked the crowd, to check on our "wife's on a mission". *"Not yet, we've got to get those picture frames"* would be the answer we got, as the afternoon wore on and on and on. Patience finally exhausted we began to plot between ourselves "methods of discouragement" we could use, to get our wife's too "let it go". We noticed when we made our visits to our wife's that the auctioneer sneered joyfully at us with his power to keep everyone under control as he carefully picked items for bid.

Corky and I determined that it was "him against us" as we were ignored by the girls each time we made a request to go home or maybe just go somewhere and buy some picture frames at a dealer's store. Corky decided to use his "maximum power" weapon of persuasion. He boldly approached Clarice and said in her ear just loud enough that it could be heard by nearby bidders

"Honey, let's go home and have some sex."

Clarice turned on him and with the fury that only a woman can muster pushed him away and declared that she intended to stay all evening if that's what it took to bid on the picture frames.

I watched the auctioneer's smiling smirk as Corky and I retreated to our station wagon vault. The next half-hour was spent exploring other possibilities such as abandonment, false fire report or "taking out" that smirking auctioneer. I finally told Corky that the best approach is the direct approach and asked him to hold the passenger door of the wagon open. I then approached Clarice, scooped her up in my arms and shouted as loud as I could "even over the auctioneer's chant"

"COME ON WOMAN, YOU GOT SEVEN KIDS AT HOME THAT NEED SUPPER," and placed her squirming, kicking person in the waiting passenger seat of the wagon. My wife was mortified, and dared Corky

"Don't you even think of it."

The bidders were astonished but best of all, that smirked auctioneer lost some of his power of hypnosis.

You must know my good friend Clarice to appreciate how determined she can be. She has never forgiven me for spoiling her opportunity to own some old picture frames. My wife has used many following years collecting picture frames as suiting punishment for my discretionary, but forceful method. A woman's scorn is bad enough but doubling your punishment is foolish and costly.

The Stinky Hitch-Hiker

One cold January evening in the early seventies a friend of mine, Jack McGregor, called me to ask if I could help him get his dead car a few blocks to a service station. His car was stalled on Tienken road about four blocks west of Rochester road. My pickup truck was fitted with a front mounted spare tire which made it easy to push him a few blocks or so to the corner, turn to the right around the corner on Rochester road and then about four blocks to a service station.

The plan was to get up enough speed to allow him to turn the corner by coasting. Then I was to line up behind him and finish pushing straight ahead. Everything was going according to plan but as he coasted around the corner and slowed to a stop, a hitchhiking hippie standing on the street corner was overjoyed for what he thought was a ride offer. My friend's car slowly stopped, and the hippie jumped into the passenger seat. I then came around the corner and lined up on his car for the rest of the push.

Meantime my friend was arguing with his odious passenger and gesturing thru a frosty window, which I mistook as a signal to proceed with the push. As he continued to gesture thru the window frantically trying to get me to stop pushing, I thought he was signaling to speed up so I accommodated him with more speed. After a few frantic blocks my friend coasted at high speed into the station and upon skidding to a stop ejected himself from the smelly car along with his grateful passenger and proceeded to chastise me while his grateful passenger was overjoyed with the ride and offered a friendship hug.

Admission Required, Pay-Up

Betty has always been an "antique nut" and she operated a store known as "Y" Knot Antiques in a small building overlooking a lake on a sparsely used road. She had accumulated several very nice furniture pieces and much delicate glassware. I did most of the repairing as required in our garage at home. Betty has always been a natural born sales person with a strong desire to please a potential customer while making a profit. Her location out on the lake was hard to find and she wanted a better location. We discovered a much larger building for rent in what was known as Keatington Antique Village.

William Scripps (long since deceased) had originally acquired 3000 acres of land in the 1920's by buying small farms and homes in the area with the intention of returning the land to nature and farming. He had built large barns for dairy and machinery housing as well as six small homes to be used for tenant workers. He also built a small school house for the tenant's children. The Scripps property with large lakes, renewed forestry and open-ness became available (after WW-2) as a plan to develop all 3000 acres into the largest new town in the USA.

The barns and all the tenant homes had been refurbished and were being rented to small business owners in Keatington Antique Village. The building Betty located was formerly used as a large cattle barn with hand hewn beams, giving it a very nostalgic atmosphere. It was perfect for an antique shop since its location was in the middle of the quaint village that had a potential to draw customers enjoying the unusual.

We moved everything in very carefully only to realize that the "Village" drew considerable people, many of whom brought children. Betty had many pieces of antique glassware displayed on table tops and in shelving which gave her concern about the possibility of breakage. She came up with a plan to reduce this liability. She decided to charge an admission to browse in the store since most actual purchases were few out of the many casual lookers.

I built a coin box on a pedestal that she placed just inside the door and affixed a sign "ADMISSION .25 CENTS". This worked very well since most kids were not that interested in the merchandise. Betty being the sales person she was, would make selected persons feel special by offering "free" admission.

However, one day a tall well-dressed gentleman walked in the door and by-passed the admission box. He seemed mostly interested in the overhead hewn beams, so Betty approached him and proceeded to make him aware of the admission cost. He very politely returned and put a coin in the box and proceeded to examine the posts and beams while ignoring the antiques. Betty finally decided to ask him

231

if she could help him find something, and he
condescendingly replied that he Mr. Keating owned the
Village.

Chapter Twelve:

Uncle Bobs General Store

Never Give In

Betty and I were having lunch one day in the Antique Village full service restaurant known as The Bull Pen operated and owned by a friend of ours. We could hardly avoid overhearing a conversation at the next table about the General Store owner not paying attention to his store manager and the effect it was having on other village store owners. We decided to contact the owner to find out if he would be interested in selling out to us since Betty's Antique store had been gaining popularity with visitors. We were certain that we could expand the store into a gourmet food shop of specialized imported cheeses and imported wines just beginning to become popular.

I had what I thought was nearly inside information concerning the 3,000-acre future for the Keating New Town development already under way. His plan included fly-in home sites as well as commuter rail service into Detroit as well as office and industrial building sites. I felt this was a great opportunity to grow a specialty business in a nearly captive upper class community development.

A purchase deal was struck with the General Store owner (Poor Richards) who already owned a successful liquor outlet in an upper-class neighborhood. Betty and I operated the old-fashioned country store in the 70's as Uncle Bob's General Store at Keatington Antique Village in Lake Orion MI.

The building was one of the oldest in the village and had originally been used by William Scripts to house his champion draft horses. It still contained mangers as well as one original iron partitioned stall on the main floor. A large fireplace had been built at the far end of the main showroom area. A corner stairs led to a loft area over the main showroom and also down to the lower levels. The loft eventually became the new home for Betty's antique business. The entire interior of the main floor had been sandblasted clean and hardwood floor installed over a concrete floor.

Downstairs was a shed roofed room along the entire south side of the building which became our sandwich and imported cheese shop. The basement area was built of natural stone walls and had a passageway opening into the sandwich room. I built unique wine racks for displaying labels of the wines which were positioned on their sides.

We had negotiated the food serving rights with Keating for the entire village except for the formal Bens Bull Pen restaurant. Our main-line menu was "ham-n-cheese" sandwiches made on homemade breads baked on the spot. The sandwich shop located on the south side of the building and consisted of a walk-up carry-off window since the surrounding grounds were furnished with picnic tables. Several times during the summer months the merchants in the village sponsored gatherings such as craft shows, art shows and festivals.

We participated in these events since it was very good for our business, but the committee who headed up the art show preparations were never happy because we retained the food service. They continually wanted to bring in food vendors in wagons to sell hot dogs or popcorn which of course would cut into our food service business.

One year a very intense effort on the part of the Art committee had enticed some rather highly recognized local artists to exhibit, and the show was touted to attract thousands of people. One of the artists was a retired VP from a major steel producer and he personally asked me in privacy if I thought we could handle the food needs of the crowd as well as the needs of the exhibitors.

He liked my positive attitude when I assured him we could handle all the casual food needs. When show day arrived we had prepared very heavily with food for the crowd. We printed an informal menu "ordering slip" with prices, which we delivered to each of the exhibitors as they set up their exhibits.

Betty had hired several young well developed young ladies wearing a skimmer hat (like my logo hat) to continually cruise the exhibitors, as runners and ask if they needed food or drink. I hawked over the public address system fresh bread or fudge coming out of the oven or the fudge cooking pot. These tantalizing odors wafted their way over the exhibitor areas and created a certain desire as planned. The girls brought orders to our kitchen help, paid for the order with "start money" and delivered the food or drink to their exhibitor customer and almost always received a nice tip. We were happy, the girls were ecstatic and the exhibitors didn't even have to leave their booths.

Late in the afternoon I decided to cruise the exhibitors too measure their show success. I came upon the VP artist and received one of the most complimentary statements for our job done that I remember. His statement was:

"Uncle Bob, You, trumped em with a duce - it was a hell of a _food_ show!"

Incidentally other ongoing efforts on the part Art committee to hack into our food shop business was attempted when a beer tent (fenced per Michigan law) was set up on the picnic grounds near our store walk-up window. A local pizza shop attempted to deliver directly to the beer drinkers inside the fenced area, but our homemade sandwiches were so popular that he gave up within a couple of hours and went back to his shop. This was during one of the "Do-nut" festivals that took place several years sponsored by the Lions Club. We worked hard at serving good quality and service for which we are still reminded occasionally of when meeting previous customers.

The (New Town) by Mr. Keating was adept at obtaining financial development assistance based on timed schedules of performance. The inability of the local governing commission to recognize an importance of a timing factor resulted in failure for what could have been. Uncle Bobs growth and success was also dependent on a New Town.

Penny candy room over here

Wine and cheese over this way

Street entryway

Penny Candy brought many kids (and parents)

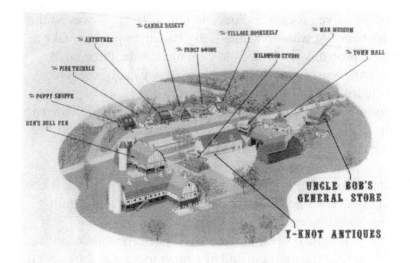

The Candle Basket
The Artistree
The Village Bookshelf
War Museum
The Fancy Goods
Wildwood Studio
Town Hall
The Pink Thimble
The Poppy Shoppe
Ben's Bull Pen

UNCLE BOB'S
GENERAL STORE

I-KNOT ANTIQUES

ANTIQUE VILLAGE

Jeanie's Listening Device

Having your own business is somewhat rewarding however you must be ready to accept long hours and inconveniences. Our teen age kids at home were on their own for a few hours after school and sometimes week ends while we ran our store. Our oldest daughter Jeanie has always been a social bug inflicted with "talk-id-ness" on the telephone. We insisted that telephone conversations were to be short since many times we needed to call home and direct home chores. Betty complained several times to me that the telephone was busy- busy- busy and she was not able to instruct dinner preparedness or check if the dishes had been done or many other motherly concerns.

Since there were five kids sometimes at home when we were away it became necessary for me to conduct an investigative process and questioning as to "who was on the telephone" at whatever time Betty had attempted to make a call. I probably don't need to explain that the three boys were the least likely suspects since they usually spent most of their time down by the creek in the back yard or were fooling around with a go-kart in the garage. This left the two girls as being the most likely, but I needed to gain evidence so Betty and I began to listen very carefully to dinner conversations especially school acquaintances and interactions that might require telephone connections. It was finally determined that our oldest daughter was the guilty telephone abuser.

I warned her that there would be repercussions if she was indeed the problem and of course there was the expected denial and self-righted ness proclaiming. I accepted her defense pleadings and another week passed by with a slight amount of improvement in telephone connectedness. Then things regressed back into the busy – busy – busy each time Betty attempted to call home, but this time Karen was at the store with us giving pony rides and Jeanie was supposed to be home with some kind of school work. The telephone abuser had been caught.

My fix for the situation was to simply remove the inside piece (about the size of a half dollar) from the voice side of the telephone thereby allowing **reception only** of a call while preventing acceptance of her voice. It worked like a charm.

Karen's Goldie

When Karen was about eleven years old Betty and I were in business known as "Uncle Bob's General Store", which was a seven day a week task for us. We were concerned about our children being home alone especially

240

week-ends in our home in Rochester. Our store was located in the country in a remodeled horse barn of the original Scripps estate from the roaring 20's. Along-side the store was a very nice two-acre chain link fenced pasture, where we were able to keep horses for our girls. Karen had a little Shetland buckskin gelding pony which had been named "Goldie" and Jeanie had a pony named "Peanuts".

Goldie was a perfect size for Karen at that age since he was short, sturdy, gentle and just a bit headstrong. We had obtained him from a neighbor about five miles from our store, but had no way to transport him to his new home. I had built a nice pick-up camper for us, complete with carpeted floor and all the necessary appliances for comfortable living away from home on the road. I decided that if we could get Goldie in the camper, we could get him to the pasture quick and efficiently. We were successful in convincing Goldie to get in the camper and Karen rode the way with him holding his tail down just in case he felt "the need". Every-thing went according to plan and Goldie soon became an attraction for the children that visited our store.

Betty and I decided that the two girls needed a weekend job, so we could keep track of their activity's. It was decided that they could give pony rides to kids that were at the store with parents. The girls were excited with the prospect of becoming wealthy by being in business. Every-thing went fine the first year or so, but the wealth didn't materialize as quickly as expected. As time passed the pony ride business deteriorated from dreams of wealth into a "demand mode" from the store management (Mom) since repeat customers were asking *Where is the pony ride girl?"*

The rides were given by the girls leading and walking the full length of the pasture and return for fifty cents. When the day presented several ride customers the job could get tiresome. Goldie seemed to get tired of his job also, especially after several rides he had learned to object by biting Karen on the butt in protest. We were never able to convince Karen that this was only one of the risks of being "in business".

Flame's Itchy Butt

After 3 or 4 years of the "pony ride" business for the girls, other interests had developed especially for Jeanie since she is older than Karen. Strangely this new interest was "Boys". Jeanie's horse named "Flame" was a full size horse and she was as gentile as she could be. Her life was pretty easy and she had been a good business partner for Jeanie. In fact, the horse-back ride business had been good enough money earned and saved to purchase a round trip airplane ticket to St. Louis for her to visit with our Valvero friends.

I need to digress a bit here involving me, Vernon Valvero and Jeanie's natural inborn love for animals. Vernon has an intense characteristic for neatness and I not being quite as blessed has from time to time furnished material for pranks on each other. I don't remember exactly how this evolved except that I prevailed upon Jeanie to present Vernon's kids with a pet Parakeet knowing full well that the resulting messiness of seeds on the floor would very likely antagonize Vernon. Strangely and almost disgustingly Vernon fell in love with that bird and it became nearly his private pet.

Any way after Jeanie's almost perfect travelers experience she seemed to blossom out into maturity and her attentiveness' to "Flame" waned. One Sunday she showed up at Uncle Bob's in the afternoon accompanying a young man driving his bright orange elevated pick-up truck.

Sunday's were always busy with visitors to the Village, consequently considerable parked cars surrounded our store.

This young man had undoubtedly spent considerable effort and money on his truck and he cared not to park his vehicle of love near other cars. Jeanie wanted to show him around the Village so she suggested that he could simply park his orange truck in the fenced pasture formerly used for pony rides but now simply occupied with contented horses. He was not as sure as she as to the wisdom of this parking arrangement, but she assured him the horses were gentile pets and nobody else would be able to park near his truck.

The gate was opened so he parked on the green grass pasture and they soon parted for a walk around to the various shops. Probably an hour or so had passed before they decided to get in the truck and leave. Upon approaching the gate they were flabbergasted to see "Flame" leaning her butt onto the bright orange passenger door of the truck and was rubbing up and down likely thinking this would cure an itch. The young man nearly passed out after looking at the huge dent in the door and promptly dumped Jeanie as he departed in disgust.

Wild Women Wine Tasters

Pontiac Michigan was basically a General Motors boomtown in the seventies. Betty and I owned and operated Uncle Bob's General Store about 4 miles outside of the city. Our store was mostly a gourmet food and wine shop enhanced with a few impulse items catering to those seeking fine imported cheeses and wines. Underneath our century old building was a beautiful stone walled wine cellar stocked with several hundred imported (mostly French) wines and from around the world. I had built horizontal wine display racks that held the wine bottles lying sideways displaying the beautiful worldly labels created by vintners while protecting the wine corks and contents from atmospheric exposure.

I had made considerable effort to study written materials as well as attending professional wine connoisseur's educational class's in order to guide my customers into a little known life style of fine wine appreciation. The unfortunate lingering after effects of the Prohibition Act of earlier years had resulted in not only the destruction of vineyards as well as a much touted ignorant propaganda against consumption of wines. There were few wine producing vineyards in the USA as a result. I attempted to place wine in its rightful place of food since the process of fine wine creation is not dependent on cooking, brewing or combining with any other process than what mother-nature had provided. My sincerity apparently had been noticed since I found myself being requested to conduct wine tasting groups with the primary purpose of world wine exposure as well as the development of tasting qualities.

After having conducted a tasting for several distinguished groups such as Prosecuting attorneys, Federal Bureau Investigators and an Exclusive Golfers association I was contacted by the Vice President of the General Motors Girls Club. She indicated there would be approximately 100 women in attendance and that they would appreciate a discussion of wines from around the world and how to appreciate the various flavors. I explained that I could serve that many using six tasting glasses per person. The tasting session was to be conducted in a meeting hall on a main boulevard just out of downtown. She asked if I could bring several cases of the wines likely to be favorites in case some of the girls wanted some to take home. I informed her that it was against Michigan law for me to sell alcoholic beverages away from my State licensed store, so she agreed to pay me up front out of club treasury for an educational program centered on fine dining. This was a bit of a stretch but she assured me that she could collect back as long as each fine dining item was marked as a food lesson in round numbers of approximate value.

The table places were set with six each of my 4 oz. tasting goblets and I was provided with volunteer servers instructed to pour not more than 2/3 in a glass since this was truly a tasting session. Empty Styrofoam coffee cups were set at each place for the purpose of expectorating as well as an accompanying cup of water intended for palate cleansing between wines. The introduction was made and I proceeded to present what I considered a few words of introduction concerning wine from a Vintner viewpoint as well as the Vintner's effort in producing an exciting food for enhancement of fine dining. My wines had been lined up behind the speaker's podium in the order of presentation first one through six and the servers had been instructed accordingly.

After what I thought was a brief introduction I intuitively sensed restlessness so I called for the first wine to be poured. The servers started in the back of the audience and part of the persons in attendance had been served before I was aghast to see they had poured the sixth or final wine instead of the first. It was a sweet desert wine intended for the finish of a meal and is nearly accepted by all being an enjoyable sweet wine. A bit of process discomposure began to prevail as I explained the error urging them to expectorate and cleanse their palates for what had been intended to be a first presentation of a robust dinner wine from France.

Deaf ears permeated the audience and I immediately thought of mothers attempting to dissuade many children visiting our penny candy shop. Having suffered an uncorrectable situation, I pleadingly restarted the session with a hearty red wine definitely intended to accompany red meat of choice. I moved on to a lighter dinner white and then a rosé, but it became increasingly clear that this crowd was not necessarily interested in the food accompaniment aspects of wine. Next was an <u>Auslese</u> from Germany which revitalized the unintended sweet mistake and proof of error became increasingly noticeable since I was having difficulty speaking over the multiple conversations and hilarity. The servers were no longer able to pour only 2/3 of a goblet but were increasingly pouring into the intended expectorating cups.

The lady Vice President interrupted my blatant boisterous presentation ---

All right you broads, you want to learn --or get drunk?

Little doubt was in my mind since the conversational din was only slightly reduced. The Vice President insisted wine glasses be gathered back in boxes. She gave an appreciated applause joined by all for my dining appreciation which I acknowledged. I asked the servers to place the boxed wine tasting goblets by the door for me. The Vice President issued bottles of wine as attendance prizes and I departed as quickly as possible after I overheard a rather buxom lady tell a couple of friends that if they would hold me, she would abuse me. It's no wonder they had a President of Vice.

Some Things Are Not for Sale

Some-time in the late 70's we owned and operated an old fashioned store where predominately gourmet foods and impulse gift items were for sale. We worked many hours including most holidays since our store was an attraction, especially when most other people were off work or just looking for a pleasant place to browse in an old fashioned atmosphere. We baked home-made bread every day in an oven that had rotating shelves in front of a window so that customers could watch as the bread loaves were baking, very similar to cookie shops in some malls.

One Thanksgiving Day we were working as usual. Since Betty would have no chance to bake a pumpkin pie for dinner at home later that evening, she had brought all the pie condiments to the store. She had put the pumpkin pie on one of the rotating oven shelves along with the bread loaves to bake.

A gentleman customer had bought several cheese's and was waiting for one of the hot bread loaves to come out of the oven when he told Betty that he wanted that pumpkin pie also.

Betty explained that it was not for sale and that it was for her own family that evening. He was convinced that it could be bought with a little monetary persuasion and offered her ten dollars which she refused with a smile. He then offered to double his offer and again she firmly stated that some things could not be bought. While his bread loaf was being packaged, and his purchases being totaled he insistently commented that money could buy anything and offered $40.00.

Betty was tiring of the situation and one last time refused to sell that pumpkin pie for any amount of money. I was entering the cheese shop at that point and overheard the refusal which I had trouble rationalizing.

But when I got home that evening and ate that pumpkin pie, it occurred to me that every-body should consume an outrageously <u>expensive food at least one time</u> in their life.

The Candy Shop

Probably a most impressive area at our General Store was the candy shop especially for child size customers since it occupied an entire room dedicated to "sweet tooth" addicts. An antique showcase was filled with box after box of "penny" candy of every color and description imaginable. The front and top of the candy case was glass covered in keeping with its intended use in the old days to separate a buyer from proprietor who would have normally been behind the case in those days. We decided to remove the sliding doors on the proprietor side and invite children to go behind the counter and fill a paper bag with penny candies of their choice. We found out on our opening day that this was a labor intensive system since the candy selection of each child (or an adult in relapse mode) had to be counted, and we soon counted by weight.

In addition to the candy counter we had one wall covered with barrels of wrapped candies as well as licorice ropes and lolly-pops. We installed a fudge cooker complete with a glass enclosed work counter where the hot fudge was cooled and cut into show case sizes. When a fudge batch was cooked and cooled the aroma wafted its way over the entire store as well as out-side the building. This enticement as well as the bread baking aroma from downstairs made our store practically an entrapment for any one with low hunger resistance.

The candy room likely was one important means of customer draw due to the intense pressure children can exert on parents as we were made aware of many times. It should be pointed out that I had installed two outside public address speakers directed to the rest of the village. Especially during weekends and various village shows I would "hawk" hot fudge or bread nearly always with the enticement of *"ARE YOU HUNGRY"*. My girls still wince when I jokingly drawl this out for them since they were subjected to this pitch over and over while they were busy and tired giving pony rides to kids.

The store front was about three hundred yards away from a very large inland lake of probably fifty acres in size. The opposite side of the lake was surrounded by new homes in what was known as Keatington New Town and residents used it for boating in summer and ice fishing in the winter.

The lake was frozen solid when this incident took place being in the middle of a winter afternoon. Betty looked out the door to the parking lot to determine the source of an unfamiliar sound. Just above the door glass was a child's head struggling with the door. Betty came from behind the counter and opened the door to discover a little boy holding a child school lunch box. His winter coat was wide open and his sock cap was barely on his head and he was obviously cold. Betty invited him in and glanced around the parking area for a parent or at least a car. She asked him if he was cold and he answered *"Yeah little bit"*. She asked him where he came from and he pointed at the lake while making his way to the penny candy room. He came from the room with a bag filled with candy and opened his lunch box which Betty noticed already contained a poorly wrapped sandwich.

Still there was no sign of accompaniment for this little guy so she asked his name which he gladly answered, as he informed her that he was going to camp out for the rest of the day, but he knew he would need food later on. Betty becoming very suspicious of the situation, asked if his mother knew about his plans, *"Donna know"* was the reply, so she asked if he knew where his mother lived and he said the street name. Betty decided to divert his intentions so she asked if he would like to work for her in the candy shop for a little while re-stocking the candy case. He seemed very responsive to employment as Betty successfully searched the phone directory for that name on that street.

A phone call resulted in a harried mother showing up to interfere with the new employee job plans. She couldn't believe he had interrupted his afternoon nap to slip out of the house for a campout. He had walked nearly a mile across a frozen lake in order to obtain necessary survival supplies for camping out but had changed plans to become a candy shop employee.

Me and Fred As Groupies

Betty and I had made a good friend of our St. Mary's church priest Father Ed Johnston while operating Uncle Bob's General Store in Antique Village. He was an exceptionally good natured man and enjoyed "fun making" every chance he could. He loved to hang out at our store and many times he would jump-in and help out in the kitchen especially when a bus load of "fudgie's" descended upon us. We had nicknamed him "Fred" which was short for Father Ed. This made for a certain informal atmosphere when customers and unacquainted persons were around. He enjoyed this immensely while waiting on some-one and he was simply a guy called Fred.

Each year during the summer the Lake Orion Lions club and the merchants in Antique Village sponsored a festival which had grown to several thousand attendees'.

The festival was named "Donut Festival" and a huge donut was baked" by a local bakery to be cut and shared by the attendance. So much fanfare had been generated after a few years of publicity that one year a country music star was invited to entertain.

Fred showed up at the store and invited me to accompany him around the festival grounds just for the fun of it. Although we were quite busy Fred convinced Betty that it would be good public relations if "Uncle Bob" would visit some of the vendors and entertainment booths. One of the first booths we came upon had bright red cowboy hats available, so we each purchased a bright red cowboy hat. This of course provided the two of us with hilarity and the courage to show off.

A country music star (Michigan's Minnie Pearl) was conducting a show on an outdoor stage and many festival attendees were gathered and gaping at the pretty lady singing love songs. Fred urged me to come right up front in our red hats and take in the pretty lady's talent. After a song or two she retreated back behind the stage to her motor home. Fred felt that since we were likely outstanding admirers of her talent that we should flatter her by asking for an autograph on our bright red cowboy hats.

We approached the big air conditioned motor home and boldly knocked on the door fully expecting to have our singer star answer. Instead some husky guy appeared and merely said

"Yeah?".

Fred said that we were great fans of (name withheld) and could she come out and autograph our red cowboy hats for us as we held them up. He simply reached out and took both cowboy hats while saying

"Wait here."

He then retired to the inside, closing the door behind while we stood looking forward to (name withheld) bringing our hats out. Instead after several minutes he reopened the door, presented us with our autographed hats and said
    "Thanks fellas, see you at the next show"
as he retreated back into the air conditioned motor home.

The Serenade

Myself, Betty and our friend Barbara enjoyed Friday night karaoke singing at Rip's bar and lounge in Pontiac. We were sitting in a booth near the bar when a patron with considerable joy-juice under his belt decided to romantically serenade the two girls, especially Betty. He made a request to the piano player and as the music started to play he stood at the end of the table and began to croon with arms outstretched "I can't stop loving you, I've made up my mind etc. etc.". Just as he was really putting all the drunken feelings he had in the serenade, out popped his teeth on the table. But not to be deterred he recaptured his distraction and finished the first few lines before retreating to the bar to plan his next approach.

Betty and Barbara snickered many times about this guy and his approach to my wife and friend, but I have never been able to see anything funny about the situation.

Fake Husband

Myself, Betty and our good friend Barbara were up north MI bumming around and generally enjoying the shops in Traverse City. Barbara was an avid collector of candles, especially the special shapes and forms that had very little utility use. She owned a small gift shop and stocked it with treasures of fancy and had given many items of this kind to Betty over the many years of our friendship. It was always my perverted pleasure to make light of these treasures in a purely joking manner since she was good-natured and seemed always to enjoy my creative harassment.

We discovered a fairly large shop this day specializing in candles and many other items of fancy. The girls jokingly requested me to stay in the car since they claimed I had no appreciation for the better things in life. I followed them inside anyway and just sort of hung back while they scattered around the premises. Barbara settled in on an exceptionally complicated candle arrangement depicting a forest with animals and trees.

I noticed a perceptive sales clerk homing-in on Barbara, so I quickly devised a plan to make a joke of the situation at hand. I quietly approached the two, just in time to hear Barbara comment

"That is the most gorgeous candle in the shop, how much is it?"

I immediately spoke to her in a gruff and loud voice

"Come on, 'honey' you've got enough of that stuff at home now."

Barbara's face fired for the first time I had ever seen and as she exited the shop in a huff, I overheard a couple of ladies comment

"How would you like to have one like that at home?"

Chapter Thirteen:

Friends and Acquaintances

Pigs in a Poke

Betty and I had bought acreage property in Metamora and had built a barn which contained a 10 X 10 stall for the horse we were intending to move from our store location in Lake Orion. We had begun to clear brush, trees and prepare a garden spot. We had made several plantings of a permanent nature and visited the site of our future home nearly every day to keep a watchful eye on everything. Our garden had been planted and most everything was growing to expectations but we began to notice several plants were being destroyed each day and many spots of excavated soil were showing up. We had no fences anywhere to protect our plantings and there were no neighbors near, but I had determined that the damages were being created by hogs.

Since I had been raised on a farm, I was very familiar with the rooting damage that hogs could create, however there was no sign of a hog anywhere. After a week or so, I bought a bag of shelled corn and placed some corn just outside the open barn. Sure enough, the next day the corn was gone and I thought I had gotten a glimpse of a pig retreating into the woods behind the barn.

The horse stall was equipped with a self-locking gate, so I decided to set a trap for my unwelcome invader. I attached a rope to the bail handle of a five-gallon bucket and put some corn in the bucket. I then fastened a heavy concrete block to a rope and pulley with the other end on to the open gate. I propped the concrete block up on a stick that was tied to the corn bucket, Knowing, that greed would cause the pig to root the corn bucket around and the falling concrete block would close the gate behind him.

Next day, sure enough I had a white 40 lb. pig in the stall, but he had two accomplices on the outside of the gate trying to console him in his trap. I was faced with the dilemma of keeping my gain or release one and try for three. The next weeks were filled with disappointments of one pig in and two out or two pigs in and one out or even no pigs in and corn all out. Finally, after several bags of corn, I had all three criminal pigs incarcerated.

I then began being a pig farmer while we ran newspaper ads and asking around the neighborhood, but nobody would claim my root-r-uppers. After a month or two of feeding and watering these stinking guests, I located a slaughterhouse that would reduce my catch into a more manageable form. The problem was I had no way to transport them. I was working as General Manager of a small concern in the city where we received from time to time raw materials in very large white woven bags about five or six feet in diameter. I prevailed upon the receiving clerk to open one of these bags carefully and save it for me.

I left my car at the plant and drove the company van home one night with my big bag and a plan in mind for my pigs. I told Betty and her sister to come out to the farm with me and that I was going to "bag" some hogs for the butcher. The plan was for me to put a "pig in the poke" and they were to hold it shut while I captured the next one.

Now these pigs were teenager size of about 60-gluttony lbs. with adult strength and smell. I entered the prison cell; leather gloved & huge bag in hand while they ganged up in one corner with fiery determined eyes fixed on my every move. I managed to grab my first victim by the back legs, one in each hand not realizing the strength a half grown hog possessed in his front legs while his back legs were elevated and kicking like a Missouri mule. Soon realizing that he was in control, instead of me, he began to tow me around the stall squealing with joy of power and excitement. He almost dispatched me when he made a lunge toward the wall supposedly knowing that I, being in a stooped-over position would crash into the wall head first like a Detroit Lions lineman without a helmet.

It almost worked and as I enjoyed a most beautiful display of stars, I uttered some appropriate praises and placed his squealing a-- (hams) in the big white bag. The other two cowered in a corner and I could see no less submission in their eyes as they grunted and consoled each other. I made my move quickly and captured them one at a time grabbing a front leg and a back leg at the same time. This caused them to roll-up on their back and I was able to manhandle them into the big open bag that Betty and her sister were holding.

Fortunately, when the bag was opened for the next squealing occupant, fear struck and they would run to the back of the bag and of course were unable to get out. Much shouting and instructional advice permeated the air along with the stench of excited hogs.

The next problem was to get a bag-full of pigs into the side door of the company van, however with the help of a little plywood ramp I was able to drag them into their hearse. When I arrived at the slaughterhouse holding pens, the attendant looked suspiciously at me when I told him I had a bag-full of pigs to be butchered. He then went to the side door of a very city-fied looking vehicle and when he opened the door; sure enough there were pigs in a sack charging the sides around and around.

He muttered some-thing which I didn't quite catch and told me to open my bag of tricks. I did so, and the pigs dashed for what they thought was freedom to root again. I have many times wondered if the slaughterhouse attendant ever related the true story of "pigs-in-a-poke" by some city guy and I wonder whether or not our company truck driver had noticed a new odor in his truck.

After my head healed and we had stashed the meat in our freezer we sort of forgot about the meat for some time. But the pigs had the last laugh since at least one or all of them were boars, (not castrated) the meat stunk like skunk when you put it in a pot. So it was all given a respectable funeral in the local trash collector's truck. So our losses were garden, filthy horse stall, bushels of corn, newspaper ads, daily care giving, headache, slaughtering costs and a stinky company truck.

I'm much smarter now, as a result "never plant garden in a hog pen".

Apprehending an Invader

We had bought a nice ten-acre home site in the hills and woods of the country. I was in the process of building a home and barn utilizing my off-time from work. Since the area was sparsely populated, I erected two gates across the driveway on the road and had installed a lock to prevent unwanted visitors. I had hidden a key to the gate lock nearby to avoid having to carry it or loan it to Betty or anyone wanting access.

An acquaintance was with me one time when it was necessary for me to stop by the barn and he witnessed my key hiding place. Now he had some unsavory characters for friends, however it never occurred to me that my property would be of interest to him or any of his friends. Several months had passed and this acquaintance asked once if he or his friends could hunt on my property. I emphatically refused and he seemed to understand, so it didn't register with me that a problem might develop. One of his friends owned a pick-up truck that was modified for mud bogging off-road activities and other street prowling events. It had oversized gripper tires and a jacked up suspension that would allow it to travel nearly any where he wanted to go off-road or otherwise.

One Friday afternoon, I was able to get away from work a few hours early, so I arrived at my locked front gates and searched for the key. It was nowhere to be found, so I walked around the gates with the intention of getting my bolt cutter from the barn and cut the lock. Disgusted at losing homebuilding time my mood was a little aggravated.

LOW & BEHOLD, parked right behind the barn was the monster truck with no one in sight. Several thoughts went through my mind and I decided that this crumb-bum was going to feel the long arm of the law if possible. Knowing that he would be armed, since it was hunting season I was certain, there would be no way I could convince him to remain while I obtained a law officer.

Looking at those huge tires suddenly inspired me to disable them, so I simply went to the barn, obtained my valve core removing tool and proceeded to remove all four valve cores. The monster truck and its owner were now under my control while I made a telephone call for the police. When the police officer arrived we began calling aloud for the trespasser. When he showed up his jaw dropped as the officer questioned him about his invasion of private property. He produced my gate key from his pocket and became obviously relieved when I told the officer that I wouldn't press charges provided he remove his truck.

He pleaded his case to the officer about not being able to drive away and the officer simply informed him that he would call for a towing service. I let the crumb-bum squirm for a little while and then handed his valve cores and told him I would let him pump air with my compressor. Never saw him again!

Cash and Comfort

A few years ago (probably 1984) it was necessary for me to make a short 500 mile-driving trip through three Midwestern States alone. My driving approach (when all alone) is to do a lot of mental planning and very little concentration on any-thing other than road conditions, traffic and of course the thermos of coffee beside me. As always I had filled up on gasoline the night before and was able to hit the road fairly early in the morning. I had good driving weather and made it over into the neighboring state by about 9:30 AM and one thermos of coffee. Now this state is probably 90 % crop and farming and well known for its ultra conservative populace. That's OK by me because I like to think I am also of that makeup.

Anyway, about 10:30 am I was suddenly faced with the realization that the gasoline gauge was showing a redline condition. Desperately I began to search in all directions for any sign of life (or gasoline) or any-thing other than dirt roads with no access from the freeway. In addition to the fuel shortage problem, I was also made aware of the coffee relief situation. I am sure that I must have driven another 100 miles before I saw a welcome green federal Hi-way sign proclaiming 2 ½ miles ahead Abadopolisville (*name changed intentionally*) exit.

Immediately my rational kicked in and I reasoned that they would only put an exit where there is civilization and gasoline. As I coasted (in order to save a few drops of fuel) off the exit ramp it became obvious that nothing was to the right except that herd of Black Angus and a few crows. In desperation I turned left under the overpass and SHAZAM as big as life itself there was a single very small filling station with TWO of the most beautiful gasoline pumps I have ever seen. There were no other signs of life except a field of junk cars and trucks, but at this point I really didn't care for any more than what I had been blessed with.

Coasting into the gravel driveway, a horrible thought passed into my mind that maybe this was somebody's abandoned dream gone bad. No, by golly, I could just make out a lone face behind the dirty window peering out at me as if to question my intentions as I stopped in front of the nearest pump. The face didn't move, so I began pumping precious fuel and then became acutely aware of the other problem. I pumped $32.00 worth of gasoline, which was $4.00 more than I had put in the night before.

I then pushed hard on the jammed entry door and presented my credit card. The attendant turned out to be a very unkempt female wearing a tee shirt with some kind of feed store logo and a Woman's day magazine open in front of her. She looked at the credit card with a scowl and punched some entries into a desk calculator. *That's $34.82* she said *"You want it on a credit card?"*

Puzzled, I said that I had pumped $32.00 worth, with which she accusingly said that she had to charge more if you *"had to buy on credit."* I took the card back and while digging for a $50.00 bill I noticed a door behind the counter and inquired if I could use the restroom.

While making change for me she said rather matter of factly.

"Taint workin"

After consuming an extra ordinary amount of time to count my change she looked me directly in the eye and asked.

"Gotta pee?"

As uncomfortable as I was I answered politely.

"Yes Maim."

"Y'all kin go aroun back like ever one else does if'n you want to."

"Thank you Maim"

As I made my way around back I fully expected to see a country style out-house behind the little building. Much to my chagrin there was nothing but open fields, a roaring freeway on one side, a field of junk cars on the other and a noticeably well-urinated spot just around the corner.

Now I am a country boy and have no problems with satisfying natures call outside. However, even if I am out in the woods I will usually seek the cover of at least a sizeable tree even-though there is nothing around other than birds and bees. So I made sure that my back was turned to the freeway even though the cars were passing at 70 MPH, but it occurred to me that somebody could be working on some of those old junks, so I quickly turned (in mid-stream, so to speak) to the building. *"**Oh no!**"*

Right in front of me was a window in the building and even though it was painted glass and covered with dirt, I now realized that the attendant was probably peeking through some flaked-off place in the painted window.

I zipped as quickly as possible and rounded the corners of the building leaving as much room as practical just in case I came under surprise attack. Upon departing the driveway and heading back to the freeway I glanced back into the building and saw the attendant busily reading the pages of her Woman's day magazine.

The next few miles were consumed in thoughtful review of my latest life experience and I suppose that I would say that Abadopolisville believes in the "Cash and Comfort" approach to business.

Impersonating an Officer

My oldest daughter Jeannie, now married has always been more or less "gritty" if challenged by a circumstance. The following situation merely accentuates this characteristic.

Living in her first home which required considerable "fixer up" activity of which she was well talented to do, promoted a deep sense of satisfaction for her. Her street being a dirt road required postal deliveries to be made in a mail box out on the road.

One weekend evening while she was busy with backyard ground maintenance, she heard loud bang, bang, bang noises coming from around the front yard. Two kids were busy smashing mailbox's as one drove while the passenger was hanging out the window with a baseball bat. She watched her mailbox get smashed as they drove by, so she jumped in her car and began following them (with out them knowing because no speeding was involved).

When they had to stop at a stop sign due to a couple of cars in front of them she got out of her car and said "*You just smashed the wrong person's mailbox. I am an off-duty officer and you are in big trouble. Give me both of your driver's licenses"*. She then instructed the passenger boy to get into her car. Both boys did everything she told them to do.

263

The driver drove back to her house (like she told him to) where she told him to give up the keys to the car. She locked it immediately and left them out in the back yard sitting on a bench fighting off the terrible mosquito's that had just started swarm since it was dusk.

She went inside the house, locked the door and then started to shake like crazy because she couldn't believe what she had just done. She called the police and they came and handled the rest. She later received a Citizens Arrest Commendation from the County Sheriff dept.

Jeannie DID TELL the officer that she lied about being a police officer and he laughed but couldn't believe what she had done. He said "we NEVER get to catch these kids doing this" "good job".

Warning: Don't mess with Jeannie's stuff because she is tough.

Tough Thief

Writing this escapade reminds me of an incident that could affect Jeannie's reputation if you should apply a strict analysis of the circumstance. Our new home in Metamora was about half dozen years old and we had made landscaping progress to some extent. A couple of years previous, I had purchased from a roadside stand several peony bulbs of various colors which had been given careful cultivation attention. It was early springtime and we were favored with beautiful blooms.

Jeannie came over to our house and had admired the peony blooms on the way in. After a nice visit she decided to return home, but asked her mother if she could cut a bouquet of these for her kitchen table. Betty was very direct in her reply (NO!) since she has never believed in cutting flowers since they should be enjoyed where they grow.   Jennie challenged this as only a child can get away with claiming she would only harvest from the back side of the patch. But the few minutes of discussion resulted in re-refused permission. The peonies were on the other side of the driveway across from the bedroom side of our house at the exit to the street. Betty anticipated as only a mother can, a possible blossom theft and sure enough as she watched from the bedroom window her thieving daughter stopped her car and quickly snatched a peony for her table.

Snowshoes

This is one of my few attempts to overcome the boredom of winter weather and maybe provoke some of my acquaintances into creative advice for an aspiring fiction writer. The following information was embellished to encourage response.-----

At my age you would think I have seen and done it "all". Well that ain't exactly true so, here we go with a new experience. We had something like 16 or so inches of snow on the ground and it seemed to be adding a little more every day. The temperatures had been around zero at night and the first big snow is still with us since there was a little rain on top of it to make a nice light crust.

Any way so much for the preface, I got a set of snowshoes from Tony and Karen for my 75th birthday. There were no instructions so it was necessary for me to discover proper usage on my own. The snowshoes were much too big for my feet so I have been putting on my boots to make my feet big enough. I can't imagine what some poor unfortunate Alaskan would do if he couldn't afford boots.

Any way I started walking in the snow out back, but I had to come back to the house right away and get a broom because some of the snow kept getting on top of my new snow shoes. I would have to stop every step or two to clean the snow off, but I finally figured out a better way to keep the snow off, and that was to lift one leg up at a time and shake my snowshoe off behind me before placing it in front of me for the next step. I really couldn't make much progress so I finally decided that the new snowshoes would just have to get shamefully messed up with snow.

I did finally get to the back side of our place and I have never seen such a beautiful winter sight. All the trees and little bushes were multiplied in size and shape with the white fluff every-where.

I found out that we had a "two-pee" snow cover (you know, that's when you have to pee two times in the same spot to hit the ground).

When I finally got to Honey-brook creek, I found out that the snowshoes should have been boots or some kind of floating material since they sink right into the mud on the bottom and boy, are they hard to lift out with mud oozed on top of them. I took them off and washed them up pretty good in Honey-brook creek because I knew that Betty would be all over me if I came home with new muddy snowshoes.

I intend to go out tomorrow with them again and I think with my first experience behind me I will be able to do much better. If any of you have any helpful suggestions for me I would appreciate any help you can give me.
Bob the Bumbler

This was sent emailed to several friends, relatives, excursionists & other selected no-goods for helpful suggestions. I received only one reply from my first-born (whom I had traded to Batista in the Bahamas for a banana boat.) His reply was of no help but I can understand that, since they don't use snowshoes in the Bahamas too much.

Never been able to get much help for this kind of activity?

Antarctic Spider Sighting
(as submitted to news organizations)

Northern Hemisphere, United States of America, State of Michigan, County of Lapeer, Township of Metamora, Honey-brook Farm, 5279 Metamora road.

Sighting location has been subjected to severe low temperatures (below zero degree) and heavy snowfalls. 22, February 2008

Situation:

Having been cooped up for many weeks on end with no one other than my wife of sixty years. I decided to venture out into the outdoor wilderness. She warned me that such a venture could be dangerous since she had heard strange rumbling noises the night before as the moon was being eclipsed. I informed her that since it is now daytime and being of sound physical condition, I had little or no fear of the outdoor world. I dressed with multiple layers of clothing, gloves, cap (all electric heated) and snowshoes. Ignoring her insistence that I arm myself with a firearm I decided to carry only a camera which can be lethal if you throw it hard enough at a predator.

Accumulated snow was several feet thick but I finally managed to make it to the location of my pond. An awesome sight awaited me at that point since all the frozen ice had been consumed leaving only the bare ground surrounded by deep snow. While gazing perplexedly and readying my camera, a deep rumbling noise came behind me.

Always alert, I whirled around snowshoes and all (much akin to a ballet dancer) in spite of the several feet of snow. There before me was a rumbling Antarctica Spider creeping up on innocent song birds. I snapped pictures and retreated to my home just ahead of the ice eating spider. (see photo, ignore the date since that's the last time I used the camera)

Having not seen one of the rare specimens since my last trip to the Antarctic, I consulted the CNN weather channel for intelligence concerning the weather at the south-pole. It seems that since the Earth has tilted into the winter solstice the sun has warmed the bottom of things causing a migration of all the ice eaters to abandon for survival. Apparently they made their trip north when the moon eclipsed and the word on the street is that they will re-adjust to our climate gradually and grow bigger under environmental protection when this article is published.

03/01/2003

The Valvero Connection

Several years ago, a very good friend (Jeanie Peine), roomed and boarded with us for a while in between jobs. She located a new job as a receptionist and met a young man who she eventually married. The four of us became lifelong friends, and here are several fun incidents that have taken place over the years.

We hadn't seen Jeanie for several weeks and in the meantime she had become engaged to a young man (Vernon Valvero). Jeanie called and informed us that she intended to

269

bring him over to our house on Friday evening (for approval I suppose). After they entered the living room, I immediately sensed that he was my kind of fun loving guy. It was only a few minutes and Jeanie proudly announced their engagement. My congratulatory statement sealed my lifelong friendship with Vernon – *"Engaged? Hell I didn't even know you were pregnant"*

Shoe Fellas

One time when we were visiting with Jean and Vernon, I asked if there was good place to buy a pair of shoes in their town. Vernon announced a large shoe outlet store in a shopping mall a few miles away. The four of us went shoe shopping, but the girls had no interest in my selection process and they disappeared. Vernon said *"C-mon I'll show you where we can find what you want"*. We moved down a long aisle of shoes sort of in the back of the store and I soon found a possibility. As I was holding a shoe up for examination and discussion I noticed a young lady store clerk approaching us. I raised my voice a little and said to Vernon *"What do you think of this?"* Vernon caught a glimpse of the approaching sales clerk and with an appropriate gesture immediately replied
"Honey, put that down, you know I don't like you in that color" The young clerk quickly turned away, having decided her input was not needed.

The Monk

Vernon and Jeanie lives several hundred miles from us and they usually make a visit to us each year. One year they called and said they were leaving home for the trip which gave us a chance to prepare for their arrival. We knew arrival time from previous trips, but when they failed to show up on time, we worried that some kind of unfortunate circumstance could have taken place. Naturally, the first question when they came in was *"What in the world took you so long to get here"*.

Vernon's reply with a very somber face.

"I have become a Baptist Monk since you last saw me and we stopped at every rest stop on the way where I preached to the seculars".

Honey Your Husband

Vernon and Jeanie made a trip out of town with another couple for a weekend of fun at a very nice hotel. As Jeanie was signing the register at the receptionist's desk Vernon approached her and exclaimed in a rather loud voice *"Hurry up honey" "Your old man just came in the front door"*

Hair Restorer

My good friend Vernon is as fun loving and prankster professional as I am. We have created several impromptu pranks together like this one:

He was visiting me as I was in the cleaning up process of a rental apartment we own. The bathtub had an over amount of rust and scum to be removed. He suggested that we go down the street to the Walmart store and buy some vinegar for the job. We are both bald-headed and when we approached the checkout counter with two gallons of vinegar, I plied him with a reassurance question in a loud tone so it could be heard by anyone nearby.

271

"Are you sure this stuff will make my hair grow back?" as I removed my cap?

"Oh hell yes, look at what it has done for me" as he pointed to his bald head.

The check-out girl rolled her eyes back in her head and took my money as fast as she could.

Parking Lot Sleeper

Vernon, Jeanie, Betty and I made a weekend trip into upper Michigan vacation territory in our truck and camper. I had built the camper since we were in the camper building business at that time. The camper was special in that it had a very large picture window in the over-cab bed area. We had pretty much spent Saturday touring and had located a place to spend the night in the countryside.

Early Sunday morning Betty and I had decided to get in the cab and drive into a town for breakfast. Vernon and Jeanie elected to sleep-in while on the road. We found a restaurant, but the parking lot was full, so I parked the camper next door in a church parking lot. We knocked on the camper door and proceeded inside for coffee while they were getting up and dressed. We waited quite some time but decided to order. When the church bells began to ring Vernon and Jeanie woke up to find themselves climbing out of bed in full view of the parishioners, responding to the bells. They remained in the camper down and out of sight until we had finished our breakfast and rescued them from embarrassment by moving elsewhere.

Frankenmuth Polka lady

The small town of Frankenmuth Michigan is unique in that it has replicated Bavaria as much as possible. We (Valvero's & Miller"s) visited the beer-garden in a shaded area beside the river that flows through downtown. A very talented trio of musicians performed most of the time with Polka and song. Vernon, not being a dancer pretty much remained in his seat, but the nice looking polka lady decided he needed some encouragement to join in the fun. So she came over to our table and placed herself on his lap and sang her next song specifically for his pleasure. This was one time that I saw Vernon without words.

Frankenmuth Camera

The tourist area of Frankenmuth has an old fashioned "penny arcade" consisting of antique machines (no longer penny operated) for amusement as in the old days. Vernon approached me about a particular machine that had a miniature drag line shovel in a glass enclosure. In reach of the shovel were many various trinkets of hardly any value that you could obtain by inserting a quarter and operating the drag line in place to capture your prize. However, of great interest to Vernon was a very nice film type camera. He reasoned that he could manipulate the drag line and we would have a nice camera to record some of our fun for the day. We began "feeding" the drag line quarter after quarter and each time Vernon would claim experience would eventually pay-off.. I invested a second roll of quarters before he finally succeeded. **The coveted camera was nothing more than a child's water squirt-er worth no more than a quarter**

The Artist

We operated "Uncle Bobs General Store" in Antique Village for many years. The grounds around the Village had large trees and many outside picnic tables for the public to use. On one of Vernon's visits he decided to entertain himself by posing as an artist for the passers-by on the walking paths. Our village was an occasional visiting place for truly artistic persons. He borrowed one of Betty's sketch pads with some of her work on it and pencils. He spent many hours of conversation that afternoon with several of our regular customers. I never did know how much <u>untruth</u> "there is another word" he spread that day, but I feared that some of my customers would associate me with the "artist guy" they had met in our picnic area.

Dinner by Bob

Vernon Valvero was working on an out-of -town job in Toledo for several weeks. He had brought Jeanie and the kids along to keep him company. They were staying in a motel while he was at work, so since Toledo was only about an hour's drive to our house in Rochester they had called and asked about week-end visits. Our kids and their kids enjoyed playing together so the anticipated visits were going to be fun for all. The first week they were coming, Jeanie called a few days ahead to confirm the week-end visit invitation. I assured her that everything was fine, however Betty and the kids were out of town for the week and I was required to leave town Wednesday on business to be back on Friday evening.

Betty, being a caring wife, had prepared a very big pot of stew for me to eat while she was gone. I worked late the first part of the week and grabbed Mc'bellie banger dinners and hadn't touched the big pot of stew on the stove. When Jeanie called me, she said they would be coming in town sometime Friday afternoon, so since we never locked a door, I told her to *"just go right in and enjoy the stew"*. Not being particularly adept at cooking expertise, I had been keeping the big pot of stew on the warm stove so it would be ready to eat without waiting. Jeanie was aghast when she removed the lid and discovered at least an inch of homemade penicillin on the stew for dinner.

Apology to Jeanie Valvero

Our favorite pastime in our "adult" (*meaning no kids anymore*) years, involve a board game of Marbles which consists of boys against girls. Since there is no skill involved other that harassing each other over the moves that are dictated by a throw of dice the harassment would some-times get pretty thick. The dice throw would occasionally create an opportunity to take-out an opponent's marble and send it back to home base requiring a start-over. If by some chance a mistake move would be made it would not be unusual for Jeanie to chide me verbally. One time my competitive spirit coupled with a fair amount of male ego (especially since we boys were losing) prompted me to refer to her as
"witch face".
Now Jeanie is and has always been a beautiful woman and I must admit that, I have many times regretted my choice of words intended purely to one-up her.
Bob the huge Bumbler

Friends Herb & Kay

In the early "fifties" Betty and I bought an unfinished home just off Freidens road from a fellow worker at ACF who was over extended. Our first encounter with Herb & Kay began the first day before we were settled in from moving. The youngest of four boys at about 3yrs old knocked boldly on our back door. When Betty answered, the little guy, arms akimbo looked her straight in the eye and demanded *"dimmy a tookie"*. Betty dismissed him as only a youngster's mother can with the command *"you get out of here"*. He retreated in a huff and as we watched him leave we determined that he lived three houses up the street. Having observed several other little boys at that location our determination was "oh boy", a couple of days later Kay introduced herself and apologized for her sons cookie demand. And that was the beginning of a lifelong friendship with some of the good times remembered as follows.

Boys and Beagle

One day, Herb and Kay had gone into town to do some grocery shopping. The four boys were left in charge of the house and each other. Sometime earlier the boys had captured a wild rabbit and were keeping him in a cage behind the house. Their home was built on a hill and had a walkout basement. One of the boys proceeded to bring the rabbit into the basement and naturally it got loose. Knowing full well that Dad & Mom would take a very dim view of the situation, since they had been unsuccessful in several recapture attempts they searched for a fix. A meeting of the minds took place and the most reasonable solution was obvious. Bring in the beagle hound since every one knows they are experts at catching rabbits. The destruction that ensued is best not described again since I am not sure the boys are completely vindicated to date.

Halloween

The four of us had bonded via some home pinochle encounters at which time Herb & I were suspicious of the two girl's total honesty. It seemed that there were some diamonds, heart or other signals when it came time to bid, and they refused to accept either of us for a partner. This following story happened as a result of the girls beating us at cards, so a night out on the town was losers' penalty. The following weekend was Halloween and we decided to dress for the occasion and go "trick or drink" calling. My brother happened to be home on leave so the five of us started out just after dark. Herb decided that his brother-in-law would be a good house to hit, so we parked in the alley. Herb dressed in stuffed overalls, rubber boots with 2x4 blocks inside to make him taller and a very large pumpkin over his head. My brother and I both had white sheets and skullcaps on. The two girls said they would wait in the station wagon to see if there were any drinks offered before they would get out. Herbs brother-in-law delivered fuel oil and his wife had a beauty parlor in the basement of their home, consequently having considerable cash in the house at times. We proceeded to the front door and began pounding away with no response. We knew they were home because we saw them in the basement as we approached the porch.

Within a few minutes, two separate police cars arrived with red lights flashing and several cops running all around with flashlights. We commented that something must be going on and just stood there watching the activity.

Herb had laid his pumpkin on the porch and my brother and I had removed our sheets.

Soon one of the cops came on the porch and suddenly the door opened with brother-in-law standing back. The cop asked, *"do you know these people?"* and he replied *"never saw them in my life"*. Herb pleaded *"Its me-Its me-Its me"*. I began to envision a trip to jail until one of the other cops showed up and identified us. The five of us were released into each others custody and decided just to go to the Blue Lounge, where Herb pledged to get even by painting his brother-in-law's front door bright red.

Nearly Asphyxiated

Summertime was upon us and the two families' decided to go camping in southern Missouri on the Current River. Since there were 6 boys and 4 adults, I volunteered to borrow my Dad's truck for transportation. This was a ¾ ton flat bed International with a stock rack. We packed all the gear for the trip and I covered the rack with a large canvas leaving the rear open. Herb and I sat in the cab as we began the three-hour trip on the open hi-way. After an hour or so we decided to stop and check on everyone in the back to see if they needed anything. When we looked in through the racks all the boys were fast asleep and the two girls were strangely passive. Suddenly it occurred that the exhaust fumes (Carbon Monoxide) had been entering the canvas shelter and all were slowly being asphyxiated.

Water Rescue

That was the first close call, the next happened while we were camped out on the side of a river. Our oldest son

Gary was always the curious one when it came to creatures of the woods and waters. While the rest of us were busy with camping duties he proceeded to wander to the edge of the Currant River. This river is a beautiful clear water fast running stream that is nearly impossible to swim. He ventured too close and fell in the water edge and was quickly swept out in the currant. He was not able to swim and began to cry for help. Betty, as with all good mothers heard the cry and began running down-stream until she was ahead of Gary in the water. She dove into the currant and intercepted Gary, but was struggling to make shore against the strong currant. Luckily a john-boat with some fishermen was able to reach them and take them to safety. This was the second close call.

Uncomfortable Bed

That evening, sitting around the campfire preparing for a good night's sleep we began to blow up our air mattresses. This was a job that took a lot of effort since the air was from our own lung-power. Herb had blown up a mattress for Kay and was complaining about the necessity of blowing up one for himself. Kay kept needle-ling him about how windy he was and it should not be a great job. After considerable time his air mattress was filled but he insisted that Kay trade mattresses, but when she demanded a reason, he informed her that his mattress was too lumpy for him to sleep on since he had hiccups when he blew it up.

Careful Driver

Friday night was a time for the four of us to go out on the town (actually country) since most of the places we frequented were not in town. They were usually dance halls in small out-of-the-way places so in order to get there some driving was required. When the road crossed a railroad, Herb would always stop the car, park-brake it, jump out walk to the center of the tracks and look first in one direction then turn around and look the opposite direction. He would then return to the driver's seat while every-one waited patiently and announce *"there ain't no trains coming"*. I am not sure anyone else ever witnessed this careful driver action, but I think he would never have done this in the big town.

Herbs Companion

Any time we were out on the town Herb, would always caution the waitress who was unfortunate enough to get our table. If the waitress approached the table along-side Herb, he would shout at her *"please watch out for my pet and don't step on him"*. He would then ceremoniously claim that he always had his one-eyed pet snake with him that rode a bicycle.

House Fire

Herb & Kay's house caught on fire one winter night. While the fire truck was on the way Herb ran next door and asked neighbor Ted if he had a water hose he could use on the fire. This was a distance of probably 150' and the hose was coiled up on the lawn beside the house. Herb quickly grabbed the hose and dashed toward his burning house. After several calls to turn on the water they discovered that the hose had been frozen and as it was being uncoiled in the cold air it had broken into many separate lengths.

Singing Career Launch

At a late time in the last century I was asked to join a concert choir bunch of males and females for Community Singing engagements planned for the up-coming winter. I was pretty sure that a talent scout must have spotted me at a karaoke bar, but since their performances were scheduled to be at various church locations it was unlikely I would need to buy booze. Realizing that most successful singers like Crosby, Sinatra or many songsters started in bars, I was sure this was the beginning of fame and fortune.

We practiced forever, at least it seemed that way but it was ten weeks of precious summertime before we were to do our first show. There were only three shows but the house was always filled and I always felt that we should have kept doing this for at least a year, you know, like they do in New York just so everyone could get a chance to hear us. That Phantom guy in Toronto had been doing his show for five years and he would even come to your town if you asked him. But guess what that director (Jerry Pakala) told us the other day? He wants us to learn some songs out of another book called Oratorio Elujah which was popular way back in the 16th century. I don't know why he doesn't want to get up to date, after all we are almost in the 21st century now.

He was sure a picky guy and you might find this hard to believe but at a couple of sessions he actually got out a stick (someone called it a baton) and waved it at all us singers. Now understand he never did actually hit anybody, but I could tell he was thinking about it a couple of times. I think he is recognizing my talent because he put me right up in the front row at the second show. The other fellows in the front row were real nice to me, but the director moved me back in the following show right behind a real big guy. I am pretty sure an under-cover talent scout for Streisand or Cher had been looking me over, and they didn't want to lose me, but I am going to be hard to convince to leave these people. Faithfulness is very honorable don't you think?

I have been able to figure out a little more about being a Tenor and it looks like all the guys were called tenors because there were ten of us, but six of them sing so fog-horn-ish that I am having trouble matching what they are doing. The other four of us seem to be doing fine matching each other and I have been thinking about asking the director if he would just like to re-name us a foursome. Then again I sure don't want to antagonize him by trying to be a buttinski into his business. I almost think he wants me to help him out sometimes because he seems to be looking right at me most of the time.

The rest of us are girls (except for us tenors) and there is good talent if you want to hear real tinkle-bell singing called Soprano. A couple of them got up one time and sang all by themselves. Somebody said it was a solo but it sure didn't seem very low to me, and it sounded real-good except it was some more of that foreign language from Latin America I guess that the director likes. All them tinkle-bell singers are on one side of the group and a whole bunch of the others are on the other side called Altos. I figured out why they are called altos is because they sing very nice all-together and "alto" is just another acronym for "all-together"

Now I must tell you a little about how they had us dress for the shows. All us tenors had black limousine driver suits with frilly belly fronts. It scared me at first since I had mostly seen this kind of suits at weddings when the main guy got married. Now even though some of those tinkle-bell singers looked good, I sure didn't want another wife. I also found out why it's called a Tux. And that's because it has a big wide belt around your belly and it sure "tucks" in some of the extra. I didn't say anything about how we had to dress pretty since if you are going to sing pretty I suppose you ought to look pretty. But I think all those audience folks got an awful good deal since they only had to pay five bucks voluntary.

I think the director must have gotten some feedback about his fascination with the language because the rest of our shows were in plain words and I had not seen even one Latin American in the audience's. Any way I know my career is underway since I have been recruited to sing with another bunch called "Pistol-paliens" who do more shows for a bunch of people called Episcopalians and (I don't even carry a gun). I sure hope the money is better which is likely since they sing every week I am told.

Singers Delusion

Delusion is a mighty strong human failing, but then maybe there is no delusion on my part about my becoming a famous singer. Here is a little background first, just so you will know where I am coming from. After investigation on my own I've discovered that I am one of those 'right' brained individuals and am likely to be afflicted with a severe shortage of reasoning power when it comes to accepting the truth about what I can do. I was born when children were taught that group singing is one of the most acceptable accomplishments of human endeavor. Therefore, it is only a short step from that to fame and fortune as a singer. To solidify this, I remembered as a young elementary school student I sang songs with the other kids and the audience applauded forever. I must have been a really great singer to be applauded and praised for ten minutes mostly by Mom and Dad too.

That's me (front row middle) I must have been an outstanding singer?

Well, anyway life's journey gets in the way of your true talents sometimes and I suspect that's what happened to me. You see I have spent the last four score and more solving right brained problems for which I was adequately compensated, knowing all along of my true talent in the other brained field of singing. Opportunity to display my singing talent had come by way of an invitations to sing with concert choir groups. Since my unused talent had not been shared with the public all those years, I accepted the opportunity to be of service to my fellow mankind.

Finally, my destiny as a great singer is etched in stone and this other group indicated they were interested in my talents. Here are some observations I want to share with anyone who would like to follow in my footsteps. (*Dad always said "share your knowledge"*). The leader of this new group named me a Tenor and I could see right away my talents were obvious, but this indicated that perhaps there were about nine others who needed guidance. This group also had a leader called "director" that never faced the audience (probably bashful) so this is surely a safety precaution to show us where to go in case of an emergency. This new Director was a lady and she was just as picky as the other one, except she didn't have a threatening stick, but her facial expressions were intimidating to say the least.

This new group was part of some kind of organization called Episcopalians and the singing bunch named themselves Pistol-paliens. I suppose I could learn to carry a handgun, so this concerned me at first, but I was told that they just wanted to keep trouble down with competition groups. After we had done a couple of shows I found out we were booked pretty solid every week for Sunday shows. I still had some serious doubts about the way things were going in this "group" atmosphere but I'm sure my talent will be discovered and I will get my own show someday. Among the first things this lady leader of these Pistol-paliens said to me was" *don't be afraid of making a mistake because we all slip up once in a while*". Now I didn't take offence to that comment, but it occurred to me that she might be thinking that I could make a mistake. I know that she will soon learn about me and I can see how tough her job is by just looking around.

Practice sessions (likely for benefit of the others) were tedious and I began to understand why the director was picky and demanding. First off they gave you song books that must have been damaged in printing. All the pages are filled with horizontal lines that almost obliterate a bunch of dots and squiggles. But then the worst part was that all the words had been torn apart and you had to put them back together in your mind before you could sing them. Finally, when you figured out what the words were and you were practicing your heart out, the director would stop everybody and say "you have to do it this way or it won't come out right". It seemed like her job was to pick on somebody if she thought they were singing to high or too low when those little squiggles went up or down. Now the way I see it, you will never make production if you keep stopping all the time.

During practice she said she wanted us to take a pencil and mark in the song book where to take a breath. I didn't want to start anything with her, but I had been taking breaths' all along. I don't think she saw me because several other Pistol-paliens were breathing right along. Some of this bunch of Pistol-paliens are girls and they are just like the other bunch I sang with (they sing real tinkle-bellish) and sometimes I just want to stop and listen to them do the singing. The Director doesn't seem to like that so I just keep singing along or at least gaping my mouth when the rest of them run away from me. I have learned too "fish lip" pretty good now and I don't think it will affect my performance since she hasn't gotten on to me yet.

During the show they always pass the money plates around, but after the show they never offer any of this to us. They almost always feed us after, but I am beginning to wonder if some of these people are being paid under the table since they have been doing this show for a long time. I should have mentioned in the beginning that I would have my agent speak to her (I don't really have an agent yet), but as soon as I get one I am going to turn him loose on her after I make sure she is not armed.

Alaska for the Hardy

In year 2000 we were invited to take a cruise and overland exploration of Alaska. Looking over the sign-up list of many possibilities for entertainment, my eyes fell on an opportunity to ride a whitewater river trip in Denali national park. Since Betty was not the least bit interested in a rough and tumble ride down a rough and rocky rapid white water river I was faced with enduring the excitement alone.

Our daughter Karen and husband Tony as well as my sister Sharon and husband George were also taking the Alaska adventure, so I started soliciting their interest in the white water adventure since "sharing" is more than half of the enjoyment of an adventure. Now Karen is a real fun loving girl, but she is also sort of "citified" and has little appreciation for some of nature's blessings aside most manmade environment. In addition to her flat-out rejection of my proposed adventure she started a campaign with her mother to dissuade me of my intentions especially since 70 plus year-olds had no business participating in a possible dangerous body bruising challenge reserved for 20 year-olds.

Now I must admit to a certain amount of male chauvinism, so this well intended "love-you" plea did nothing more than fire my original desire into a full-fledged conviction that I would be nothing more than a "chicken-hearted" cowardly specimen if I failed to participate. My next effort to obtain a white water river adventure partner was Tony, but he had already made plans for a helicopter ride over the mountains which were also among some of my original thoughts, but since I had several hours of small aircraft flying in my younger days, this was rejected in favor of river-rafting.

My sister Sharon & George live in another State many miles from me, so my effort to enlist her as a participant in white-water rafting was confined to the telephone. Just so you understand I will take just a moment to explain a family heredity for playful joking others for fun and little did I realize why my sister refused to even consider riding a white-water river raft with me, but slyly suggested George as a potential partner saying I should call him in another couple of hours when he came home from work. Now George is a few years younger than me, but he is much cut from the same mold as me in many ways, so I hoped he might have the same adventure thoughts especially if we were to experience it together.

My call to George was unfortunately made at a bad time since he was exhausted from a unusual heavy day's work, so when I mentioned him signing on for the white-water adventure he simply stated a disgusted "you are out of your mind" reply. Realizing his quick refusal was because of exhaustion I diplomatically promised to hold up signing on for a few days. Having been turned down over and over I waited two days and called George again. This time he was slightly more receptive, little did I know that Sharon had been working on him thinking it was fun to see him squirm. George was not very enthusiastic when I called so he began with several imagined problems we may be getting into. I finally made a flat statement that I was signing on tomorrow and that if he didn't he would be known in my book as "chicken-hearted" from now on.

Let's jump ahead now to the early morning of the overnight lodging at Denali, we were informed to board a small bus for the white water departure point roughly a mile away. No time for morning coffee at the restaurant but we were assured of a cup from the large thermos brought on by the young driver. UHG The morning was chilly even though all the rest of our world was steeped in mild temperatures at home, but we arrived at a small departure building having had very little time to consume the Styrofoam cup of blazing hot coffee. Six people including George and I were herded into a small dressing area and issued wet suits to be donned over our street clothes. We were cautioned to solicit help in putting on the waterproof suit, since they are very expensive and can be punctured if mishandled. The six people in our group were male except one hesitant wife of one of the men who had apparently conned her into this adventure.

She hesitatingly looked at the wet suit issued to her and asked "what is this" and before thinking, I said for the benefit of the group "I think it's called a body-bag" and thankfully George bellowed laughter which sort of tempered the hesitation of the lady, I think. The six of us were assigned a rubber raft piloted by a young shapely lady who could not have been more than 25 years old. Before launch she instructed all of us of the possible hazards and carefully explained that if we encountered a collision with any thing that caused anyone to be ejected over board, the most important thing to do was remain calm and simply float until a rescue was made. George looked at me and said "look at what the hell you got me into".

Three of us were seated in the front seat and the remaining three were seated behind in the back seat. George was seated on the left while I was seated in the middle and the lady wearing the "body-bag" was seated on my right. We were instructed to hold on to the side ropes and lock arms with each other. George commented to the pilot lady, that "since I was the oldest in the group with the most life to lose please take the smooth water route". The water was unbelievably swift and seemed to twist and turn every few feet as it collided with straight up mountain rock walls. Occasionally rock walls seemed to close in on both sides of our river squeezing it into reckless flowing speed as if the river feared being closed off from its desired journey. Our front seat just a few inches inside the front rubbery extremity was expected to take the brunt of all nose-in dives inundating the three of us with ice cold water over and over. The young lady pilot stood up on the back end of the raft wielding a seemingly useless oar and yelling at us all to lean left or lean right when it appeared we were destined to collide with a rocky protrusion directly in our path of destiny. At one place in our journey I noted a railroad track high upon the side of a mountain wall over our river, supported by long very rusty columns and the remains of a fallen railroad car in our river. Nothing bothered me about this sight until later in our journey we were transported on a site seeing rail ride and a flash back memory recall of those spindly rusty columns.

The trip was exhilarating and miserably cold since the wet suit would allow a little icy water to dribble down the front just under the chin, but we arrived safely after about a two hour run. Our pilot lady beached us on a turn of the stream at a sand bar near a highway and immediately instructed us to carefully remove our so-called wet suit body bags and return to the lodge bus terminating all the river fun. We were beach seated on long wooden benches on a cloudy day that had just deposited rain on the seating accommodation. Our bus was quite a bit overdue for survivor pick up and our street clothed bottoms were rainwater wet as well as our tops river water wet. On our return bus trip I envisioned a hot shower in the room and a delicious breakfast in the restaurant. Upon arriving at the lodge we were informed that we were checked out of the room and that our next bus was waiting for our arrival to the next Alaska enjoyment for the hardy.

I'm not smiling because two people were force-ably holding me as you can see.

Chicken in a Box

Betty and I decided to take a drive up to northern Michigan for a visit with our Daughter Janene and her good-natured husband Tom. He had been transferred to a very responsible job there and had started the new town adjustment by renting a home. Living there for some time they decided to make a purchase offer on the home with thoughts of up-grading and remodeling which was well underway by this time. Readjustment to country-town living was beginning to become a familiar lifestyle and they were adjusting accordingly.

Having spent nearly all my life in country style living, I volunteered by phone to Janene to bring a couple of chickens for them to enjoy and even promised to help Tom build a small pen in the back yard. She began by thanking me for my kind considerations, however she very firmly refused the chicken offer and insisted that her town had a "no chickens allowed" ordinance. I couldn't fathom this, but decided to test her "refusal excuse" by blaming the town management. So!

I salvaged a cardboard box about "chicken" size and removed about half of the top cover flaps. I re-enforced the box with duct tape and made sure the "halved" top cover allowed room for a "mechanical engineered" chicken to flap his/her wings under a towel cover while being transported to country town existence. I removed a coat-hanger wire (never liked that shirt any-way) from the closet and straightened it out. I fished the wire thru a small axel hole at the bottom of the box at the open top end and inserted the wire across the bottom through another small axel hole on the opposite side. The shaping of the wire while in the two (axel) holes was primarily a "vie" that could extend above the open top. I formed a couple wire axels inside the box and bent a finger angle to be depressed while a tea-towel was spread over the open end of the box. It didn't take much practice to hold the chicken box while fingering the wire vie under a towel to look like a chicken in the box looking for an escape to freedom.

I left the chicken box in the car until the welcoming conversations had subsided since we arrived during the day while Tom was busy at work. This was good because separate chicken gifts doubled the fun. I then excused myself and I think Betty may have primed Janene about a gift her father had brought for her. I entered the kitchen door holding the box preciously in front of my shirt (anticipating soil) while finger flipping the vie under the towel. After asking if my chicken could get a drink of water, we (chicken & me) were evicted nearly physically from her kitchen, abused verbally. Several minutes passed before mother and daughter exited and I was rewarded with a hug and kiss (worth the effort) but daughter-like-father decided that a telephone call to Tom was in order. She proceeded to name her father as possibly causing him to get an ordinance citation. When he came home I pretended to be unaware of his un-spoken avoidance until I mentioned my chicken was outside and needed water. He then began to diplomatically refuse the kind offer. We are all good friends now and I don't think they meant it.

Red Spots

18th Mar 2017   (Betty died 3/3/2017)

I was married to my Betty within just a few days of seventy years when she contracted a mild case of pneumonia and was transported to the hospital on Tuesday 28th Feb. The first few days of hospital care indicated recovery was favorable although she refused food until Saturday lunch. My children and I were elated that she was able to sit outside her bed for this.

Everyone was encouraged, so left the hospital at visitor closing time of 10:00pm for some much needed rest. My arrival at the hospital Sunday morning found Betty in a semi-conscious condition with only an occasional awakening. My son arrived later and we were astonished at the changed, occasional alertness in Betty. He and I spent the rest of the day and well into the night before finding out that she had suffered a very hard night before.

Apparently Betty had gained enough energy from her food intake during the day to give her the strength to demand her release after our departure at about midnight. Obviously, this was denied so she made six phone calls to my phone which I didn't hear, (resulting in no response) but she also called 911 two times so, all this resulted in medical sleep attention.

Sunday a couple of remarks from Betty about some red spots on the wall and floor during an wakening at onetime in the early evening was ignored. Finally, after her repeated insistence about red spots, I asked Betty to point out where a red spot on the floor was and I said I would pick it up to show her there was nothing. She pointed and I leaned out of my chair and scooped my open hand across the floor and presented it for her. She gently touched my hand as if to take the nothingness into her hand and re-entered her restfulness.

The next two days were filled with nearly continuous visitation, for Myself, Janene, Karen and Tony, Gary and Louise with literally no change in Betty. Tuesday evening about 6:00Pm, my two daughters suggested I should eat dinner quickly at the hospital café since closing time was 7:00PM and they would go after me. I ate quickly with Gary & Tony and returned to Bettys empty room since the two girls had already left for the café.

When I opened the door, I was astonished at the sight of **countless brilliant red spots** on all surfaces of the room. My initial momentary thought was **why** did those two daughters decorate that room, but quickly walked over to Betty and proceeded to bend over and kiss her hand. When I stood up to go around the bed, **all the lights were gone**. Betty died in the next few minutes in the presence of all of us.

This has been an unforgettable experience.

The above experience has bored heavily on my mind very much as I discussed it with many acquaintances resulting in hardly no opinions, however some few had similar happenings. My seventy-year partnership with Betty was literally filled with her ability to formulate personages, characters or situations in sightings of humanity and nature. She had the ability to transfer these many times into the form of sketches and drawings. I can only wonder, had she not died that evening, would she have been able to transform this "Red Spot" sighting into sketch or drawing form for human analysis?

Our home located in a countryside consisting of large trees, wetlands, lakes, brooks and dirt road openness has always afforded our comfort and pleasure. Here is a picture example of Bettys creative attentiveness which prompted her to share with others who happened to be enjoying our porch/nature view. Her explanation of this ordinary oak-tree configuration would be to point out, at the very top are two limbs extended out as if to offer you a friendship hug while the approving head/face looks on.

These two limbs are at least 40 feet off the ground but Betty didn't seem to consider that little detail.

Made in the USA
Monee, IL
16 September 2024

65970069R00174